I0791545

A Guide To The REVOLUTION

A non-violent guide for returning our country to the human people

Shirley Conley

Archway Publishing books may be ordered through booksellers or by contacting:

Archway Publishing
1663 Liberty Drive
Bloomington, IN 47403
www.archwaypublishing.com
844-669-3957

Because of the dynamic nature of the Internet, any web addresses or links contained in this book may have changed since publication and may no longer be valid. The views expressed in this work are solely those of the author and do not necessarily reflect the views of the publisher, and the publisher hereby disclaims any responsibility for them.

Any people depicted in stock imagery provided by Getty Images are models, and such images are being used for illustrative purposes only. Certain stock imagery © Getty Images.

ISBN: 978-1-6657-0654-4 (sc)
ISBN: 978-1-6657-0656-8 (hc)
ISBN: 978-1-6657-0655-1 (e)

Library of Congress Control Number: 2021908503

Print information available on the last page.

Archway Publishing rev. date: 06/08/2021

CONTENTS

PROLOGUE

This book is definitely NOT politically correct with either party. But it IS the TRUTH as I know it to be and that my research has proven to be true. It is something the politicians will never tell you. They and the corporations owning them will discredit me and call me an idealist. But what is so bad about wanting your country to be the best it can be? Ideal means the standard of perfection and the model for imitation. Their name calling is how I know I am right. As my favorite line from the movie, "The Rage of Paris" says, "I can took it."

This book was originally looking at government as the problem. But then I realized that the problem is corporations who buy the politicians. Everything the government does is for the benefit of corporations and not human people. Even the Supreme Court gave the corporations the same status as human beings when the Republican dominated court ruled that corporations are "people" in their Citizens United decision. This book is to make corporations, since they are people, start paying their fair share and how to accomplish it. They have sucked the joy out of our lives and it is time we put a stop to them.

This book has taken me over 30 years to write. Not because I didn't know what to do, but because every time I would get it ready for publication, you would do something stupid and make me say, "Those morons aren't worth it." Then it would sit for a few more years. It survived George W. Bush, who up until now, was the stupidest President we ever had. But then you elected Donald Trump and almost re-elected him and that has pushed me over the edge. I honestly don't know what you were thinking. You elected Joe Biden, a Democrat, but took away members of his party in the House of Representatives and left the Senate in a 50/50 state. In theory having the branches of government split between parties would be a good thing to keep a balance of power. But after what the Republicans did under Trump, that is no longer a reality. They used their clout in the Senate to block everything Democrats wanted to do. Just look at what Mitch McConnell, the Republican leader in the Senate, did with the $2,000 Trump wanted to give to you, the human people. He refused to allow it. You still don't deserve this book but I am doing it because you are taking ME down with the country.

I am officially naming the period from the sixties on as the Moronic Age. Never have so many known so little. The recent violent insurrection by Donald Trump, who refuses to acknowledge that he is a loser and lost the election, is proof that this is the Moronic Age. Over 74 million people believed his lies that the election was stolen, when even the judges that HE appointed and people in charge that HE appointed say it was the most secure election ever and that he lost fair and square.

I hadn't intended to even mention Trump, but after what he has done during his four years in office, I have had to change much of what I had written to address the abuses that he committed, from empowering racists to making lying the main policy of the Republican party. The Republicans just verified what Hillary Clinton had said about Trump supporters – they are deplorables! They beat up Black Lives Matter people, caused a security guard to have a fatal heart attack at our nations Capitol, destroyed our Capitol building, and perpetuated Trump's lies. All under the name of "patriotism." Bullshit! You are not patriots. You are low-life criminals and should be locked up as traitors. Because that is what you are. There is nothing patriotic about beating up innocent people and destroying the very institution that you claim to be defending. You are ignorant terrorists and no better than the terrorists of 9/11.

On the day of the violent insurrection, Trump went on Twitter and told his goons that he would be there with them as they went to the

Capitol. But guess what? He wasn't there. He ran back into the White House and watched them demolish OUR CAPITOL and attempt to assassinate our congress people on television and was enjoying it. They had planned to murder his own vice president! But for a brave security officer leading the murderers away from the chambers, Mike Pence, his Vice President would have been dead. Trump had many, many chances to denounce and call off the murderers but he didn't and to this day would not admit he lost the election fair and square, which he did!

It is also rumored that one of the Republicans in congress gave a tour to some of the insurrectionists the day before the insurrection so that they would know where to go on the day of the attack. That Republican should be arrested, tried for treason, and executed.

I hadn't intended to get into the election but after what happened, it makes my book even more necessary because we need a way out of this without violence. Violence is only going to leave a lot of dead people and destroy the very things we hold dear in our democracy. You need to read this book and get off your lazy asses and participate in your government in a positive way and not with violence.

When I refer to some of you as morons, it is done with apologies to the true morons, who cannot help their condition. I am referring to those of you who meet the definition by way of being a "very stupid person" because you CAN learn but you just choose not to do so. I should be politically correct and refer to you as Mr. Hardy Hayes of Camarillo, California does in his editorial when he referred to you as "low information voters." Mr. Hayes nailed it. But he is much more tactful than I.

If you doubt that many of you are morons, just look at some of the things you do. There are the politicians and voters who are approving recreational use of marijuana at the same time we are dealing with homelessness and a heroin epidemic. You elected Bill Clinton and treat him as if he is a rock star when he was responsible for signing the Gramm-Leach-Biley Act of 1999 which repealed the Glass Steagall Act, put in place after the Great Depression of the twenties to prevent banks from reckless investing. The result of Clinton's action, led to the banking collapse during President George W. Bush's term. Clinton signed the NAFTA free trade agreement which created a mass exodus of jobs in the United States to other countries. Then you wanted change after President Bush and elected Barack Obama but then when he didn't fix in two years the mess Bush left the country in, you elected a Republican congress who vowed to block everything President Obama tried to do. For six years, the Republican Congress did nothing but spend your money investigating President Obama's birth certificate.

When it comes to news, you prefer Fox (Faux) News or a former drug addict like Rush Limbaugh who broadcast blatant lies. You fail to question what they say when much of it could be easily fact checked on the internet by going to reliable sites. It has been rumored that the owner of Fox News, Rupert Murdoch said about his listeners, "God bless trailer park trash and idiots everywhere. Without them Fox News would be nothing and I would not be a billionaire."

You said the government should keep their hands off your Social Security and Medicare. Social Security and Medicare ARE government programs, you morons! Then you go out and protest again against Democrats who are the very people trying to obtain benefits for YOU and not just corporations.

You are like Lucy and Charlie Brown with the football. Every election, Republicans (Lucy) tell you that they will do away with abortion and restore the "sanctity" of marriage. You elect them (kicking the football) and they never do anything for you (pulling the football away when you get near it.) You repeat this every election. Republicans will never eliminate abortion because that is the issue that draws conservatives in every time. If Republicans actually ban abortion, then they won't have an issue to draw people into their party.

You are easily brainwashed with the subliminal ads on TV. Newt Gingrich mentioned Saul Alinsky, a Chicagoan who taught the poor how to obtain government power by organizing against the Daley Chicago machine. Alinsky's "Rules for Radicals" was used by members of the Tea Party including James O'Keefe who helped destroy ACORN, the community organizing group for minorities. You believed that Obama grew up with Alinsky, when in reality, Alinsky died when Obama was only ten years old. So, I hardly think Obama "studied" with Alinsky. But hey - they were both from Chicago! Other Republicans told you Obama was part of the Daley Chicago corruption. So, which was it? Was Obama with Alinsky or Daley?

Here is the big difference between the 99% and the 1%. The 1% vote for *their* best interests. But most of you 99%-ers vote *against* your own best interests. Even today, over 40% of you say you will vote for Republicans. You have no job. No healthcare. You lost your home. What in hell makes you think Republicans are going to help you when they flat out tell you that they are going to help corporations and rich people?

You elected Donald Trump, who lied to you constantly. You could very easily look up what he said five minutes ago and see that he is now saying the exact opposite, but you still believe what he is saying now. A writer to the opinion section of the LA Times said about the border wall, "Trump should just say it was complete and his followers would believe him and the rest of us would be off the hook for the $5 billion!"

These are just a few examples of how stupid most of you are. I want to educate you. You are probably not stupid - you CAN learn. You just choose not to and that is what makes you so dangerous. If you read something on the internet, look to see who wrote it. If it isn't from a reliable source, at least fact check it before passing it along to others. Also ask yourself who will benefit from that story.

In spite of your moronism, I am going to lay out a COMMON SENSE plan for you to take our country back from the corporations who destroyed it. I am doing it, not because you deserve it because you don't. But I am doing it because you are taking me down with you. Change will come from YOU, the human people.

My suggestions may seem harsh, and they are. But when you

ignore problems for over two hundred years, the solution has to be harsh. Just like when you ignore a health problem and when it finally gets to be too much to handle, you find out it is cancer and need to have some part of your body removed and may even lose your life. The treatment is harsh but only because you ignored the problem.

INTRODUCTION

REVOLUTION: The renunciation of one government or ruler and the substitution of another by the governed.

Our revolution is not so much against our government, although that needs to happen as well, but it is against corporations. They are responsible for our national debt because they get our government into wars so they can steal resources from other countries; they cause the catastrophic illnesses that bankrupt Medicare and Medicaid; they destroy our infrastructure with their semis delivering their products; and they keep merging with other corporations which results in less competition. So called gentrification is merely a way for corporate trusts to drive the poor out the cities and turn housing for the poor into condos for the wealthy. They want to keep a certain portion of the population uneducated and poor so that they will have someone to fight their wars, mow their lawns and do other work that well-educated people will not do.

They are listening to your phone calls. They are reading your e-mails. They monitor what you buy at the grocery store. They demand your passwords to Facebook and Twitter. They know who you have sex with and probably everything you do. No, I'm not talking about Big Brother Government. I'm talking about BIG BROTHER THE CORPORATION. Even before you walk out the door of your local supermarket, that corporation knows about the case of beer and condoms you bought. AT&T knows where you are at all times if you use your cell phone. Cameras monitor you at parks, Starbucks, parking garages, and just about any business you frequent. If this sounds like something out of George Orwell's book, "1984" written in 1948, that's because it is.

If you doubt that corporations control our politicians, lookup "Business Roundtable" an association of CEO's who seek to form public policy.

Corporations hate government regulations, but love government contracts. They hide their income off shore to avoid paying income taxes at the same time as they ask the government to send our military in to protect their foreign interests. They hate welfare for you, but love it for corporations in the form of subsidies. Why should you and I subsidize an oil company when they gouge us at the pump, ravage our land by drilling and fracking, and then export the gasoline to China?

A perfect example of corporations privatizing the profits and socializing the losses is the Exide Battery plant in Vernon, California. For years, Exide dumped toxic waste into the area surrounding the plant. The homes in the area were occupied by poor people who couldn't afford to live anywhere else. Exide didn't want government regulation so your politicians left them alone to pollute at will. They were only required to put a minimum amount of money into a "clean up" fund. When children near the plant started getting lead and arsenic poisoning from their toxic waste, the plant was finally closed down. But Exide only paid $50 million toward the clean-up and in 2016 Governor Jerry Brown asked the legislature for $176.6 million for the clean-up. Trump came along and had his justice department and other departments with control over Exide's bankruptcy agreement stand back and not oppose the agreement. This agreement allowed Exide to walk away from all responsibility for the plant clean up. This is a sweet deal for Exide who pocketed the profits all those years and only paid $50 million to clean up a mess that will cost well over $176.6 million. You, the chump, will pay the rest with increased charges when you buy a new battery for your car.

WHY THIS BOOK? Russian leader Vladimir Putin said it very well when he said of the protesters (the governed) calling for a revolt of the election in Russia; *They don't have a unified program, they don't have a unified vision of which means to use to achieve their goals which they have yet to formulate, and they don't have people."*

The Occupy Wall Street protests in the U.S. only succeeded in getting Bank of America and other banks to stop charging fees to use a debit card. As far as changing anything that caused the banking crisis, Occupy Wall Street failed to achieve anything. Why? Because they REFUSED to be organized! They left such a bad taste in everyone's mouth that anything they do from now on will be irrelevant. They lost the trust of the people. So, they had their 15 minutes of fame and they blew it!

The purpose of this book is to give you, the human people, a unified program, a unified vision, and goals. As for the people, you will have to get together yourselves. I can't do EVERYTHING for you.

What I am offering here are MY suggestions for fixing our country. You may have better ideas and I hope you do. This is to get you thinking and becoming part of the solution instead of part of the problem.

I found it ironic that two people that I find helpful in developing a plan to take back our country from corporations committed despicable acts. The first person was Vladimir Putin and the other person was Osama Bin Laden. Why Bin Laden? Because he knew exactly what the problem was (the United States for invading countries, stealing their resources, and desecrating their sacred lands). He knew exactly who to go after to seek revenge (the Wall Street traders who encouraged the corporations, the Congress who enabled them, and the military who carried out the mission.) Bin Laden attacked New York City Wall Street traders, the Pentagon, and but for the heroes on Flight 93, he would have gotten Congress. I have half-heartedly joked that the real tragedy of 9/11 was that Flight 93 didn't get through to Congress. He would have done us a huge favor by eliminating all of them at once since YOU can't seem to do that by voting.

The point here with Putin and Bin Laden is that they knew the problem, what to do to solve it, and then executed their plans. YOU have to do that in order to take back your country from corporations.

The problems listed in this book are the very same problems MY MOTHER complained about 75 years ago. They have never been solved. Why? Because we only have two parties to choose from and they just go back and forth every four years. But mainly because YOU the voters don't understand how your own government works. You repeatedly elect a president because you like his or her goals and then you proceed to reelect a Congress that is of the opposite party or against the goals you want your president to achieve. We have millions of people in this country, yet we can't come up with 535 intelligent people who care about us instead of taking bribes. You just did this again in 2020. You got rid of Trump and elected Biden but then you took away some of the Democrats in the House and re-elected the two most evil members of the Senate – Mitch McConnell and Lindsey Graham. McConnell said when Obama was elected that his goal was to keep Obama a one term president. "Imodium" Mitch recently said he is 100 percent focused on stopping President Biden's administration. Now you want Biden to change things that Trump ruined but you left him with a Senate that will oppose whatever he wants to do. Then in four years when Biden wasn't able to change anything – because of YOU – you will vote for a Republican president.

I know many of you are much smarter than most of our elected representatives. For example, John Maya of Rancho Palos Verdes, California said, "We can pay everything with what we currently pay in taxes if only it was spent properly." He is so right. When our military automatically pays invoices under $1 million dollars without verification, you don't have to be a genius to know there is a problem that needs fixing.

If you don't think you are smarter than our current crop of politicians, think about one female politician who said she did not want to sit by the window on an airplane because she didn't want her hair to get blown. Honestly! Honey, if your hair is getting blown on an airplane, you've got more problems that your hair to worry about.

Another male member of Congress, when told he needed a visa to visit a certain country, responded, "No I don't. I've been there before and they take Master Card." Still think you aren't smarter?

Our current elected officials are the worst ever. Aside from their greediness, they are ignorant as well. Whatever problems they can't control, they legalize it. They couldn't control alcohol, so they legalized. They couldn't control gambling, so they legalized it. They can't control drugs now, so they are legalizing marijuana. What's next? Legalize rape and murder?

Politicians fail to consider the impact of their legislation. For example, in California, they passed minimum wage legislation. They did not consider the fact that many of the low- income earners were getting subsidies for child care and other services. However, many of these people who are getting the wage increase are losing their child care subsidy so that they are actually in worse shape financially now.

The reason Hillary Clinton lost her election wasn't solely because of Russian hacking. She couldn't relate to you and I. Both she and President Obama only came to California when they want to fill their pockets with campaign donations from Hollywood. They wouldn't even talk to the rest of us if they didn't need our votes. Once they get our votes, they forget about us. I can remember when I used to write to a politician about a problem and they would write back. Now I get an email asking for money and never hear a peep from them about my problem. They won't listen to me because I never give money to a politician. **To me, giving money to a politician is like tipping the guy who just burglarized your house.**

If my representatives had taken my advice about the mortgage crisis, we would not have been in the mess we are in today. I suggested that as a condition of bailing out the banks, the banks had to take homeowners with high interest rate mortgages and give them a 5% rate and a 40- year loan. Had they done that, people could have stayed in their homes and we would not have had the glut of foreclosures that drove down the prices of all of our homes. Had they listened to me, banks would have made more money and people would still be in their homes.

This book is offering my ideas for change. Republicans should love my ideas because they are all based on the premise that people accept responsibility for themselves. Since the Supreme Court ruled that corporations are *people*, then corporations must now accept responsibility for their actions.

We must eliminate the policy of corporations *"privatizing the profits and socializing the losses"* as talk show host Randi Rhodes said. Corporations don't want to be regulated and don't want to pay taxes. But when they get in trouble, as the banks, airlines, and General Motors did, they want to "socialize" their losses by having you and I bail them out from their incompetence. That has to end. The Republicans made it easier for corporate people to file bankruptcy while making it harder for you to do so at the same time. YOU must pay a portion of your debt, but corporations get away with avoiding responsibility, like what is currently happening with Exide. Trump's Attorney General did not oppose Exide walking away from their debt in their bankruptcy filing.

"Never doubt that a small, group of thoughtful, committed citizens can change the world. Indeed, it is the only thing that ever has." Margaret Mead, American anthropologist.

In this book I am attempting to educate you and offer suggestions to fix our country. I use humor to make your journey through this book an enjoyable one. But the problems are serious ones so don't think that the humor minimizes the seriousness of the problems. It's just to make it easier to understand. I am writing the book in plain language that even the morons can understand. I know the big words but what good is using them if I can't get my point across to everyone? This is a problem with professors and attorneys. They want to impress you with big words. But what good is it if the people you are trying to teach can't understand what you are saying.

As Joseph Pulitzer said about writing, *"Put it before them briefly so they will read it, clearly so they will appreciate it, picturesquely so they will remember it and, above all, accurately so they will be guided by its light."*

WHAT HAPPENED?

"I see in the near future a crisis approaching that unnerves me and causes me to tremble for the safety of my country...corporations have been enthroned and an era of corruption in high places will follow, and the money power of the country will endeavor to prolong its reign by working upon the prejudices of the people until all wealth is aggregated in a few hands and the Republic is destroyed." These words were supposedly uttered by President Abraham Lincoln on November 21, 1864! However, claims were made that they were forged by his private secretary, John Nicolay. Whether Lincoln actually said them or not is not the point. Someone recognized the problem in 1864.

Guess what? The quote was right and the prediction came true! Now what are YOU going to do about it? Yes YOU. Because YOU ignored the problems for years and YOU never questioned authority. YOU allowed the media to repeat lies without calling them on it. YOU allowed your so-called representatives to lie to you over and over and YOU just kept re-electing them. YOU failed YOURSELF and the rest of our country with your indifference. Edmund Burke, a Scottish philosopher said, *"All that is necessary for the triumph of evil is that good men do nothing."* Most of you do not exercise your right to vote. If you don't vote, then you have no right to complain.

French author, Voltaire said, *"Those who can make you believe absurdities can make you commit atrocities."* The evidence is again shown by the Tea Party members who were fired up by the corporate lies spread by the likes of Sarah Palin, Rush Limbaugh, Michelle Bachman, and others recruited by Freedom Works and Donald Trump. They repeated the corporate lies so many times on so many media outlets that YOU accepted them as truth. There is no excuse for your behavior because you can research anything instantly on the internet by going to trusted sites. Ask who is funding these movements and who is funding the studies and what they have to gain.

Corporations were clever to conceal their identity and their involvement in issues. Congress is bought and paid for by corporations. YOU allowed 9/11 to give corporations and the government the right to trample your rights with the patriotic sounding legislation like the "Patriot Act" or the "Prescription Drug Benefit" or "No Child Left Behind." The only problem is that the Patriot Act allowed corporations to listen in on your phone conversations. The Prescription Drug Benefit prohibited Medicare from negotiating for better prices for the patient's prescriptions. No Child Left Behind left all their behinds behind and somewhere there was probably a corporation that benefited from the testing programs or charter schools.

Did you know that very few of your legislators write the actual legislation that they propose? Corporate lobbyists write most legislation and simply present it to their shill in Congress who then brings it to the floor of Congress. In return, your representative or his family members receive some benefit from the corporation - either campaign donations or donations to the member's own charity. Call it what you like, but it is a bribe!

Your representatives are like Lucy when Desi confronts her about blackmailing him.

Desi says, "That's blackmail"

Then Lucy says, "Let's not call it that."

Desi says, "Well that's what it is."

Lucy says, "Well I know, but let's not call it that."

We know it's a bribe but let's call it a donation or campaign contribution.

You have to understand the role corporations have played in our country and why the United States is hated in many countries. First, and this should be no surprise to anyone, is that the United States "takes" whatever it wants in the world because of corporate interests. Oil companies want the oil in the Middle East so they staged a war and took it. Donald Trump is probably the only person who spoke the truth about our interests in Iran when he said we should go into Iran, destroy them, take the oil and get the hell out.

Since our country was founded by taking the land from the Indians and later the Mexicans, it shouldn't surprise you that we are seen as the bully in the world. Our need for a military is mostly to protect corporate interests in other countries. We have no other reason to be there but for the corporations who have offices there. Do you really think Dick Cheney cared whether or not the people of Iraq had a democratic government?

Just recently President Trump brokered a peace deal with Israel and Bahrain. Why does he care about Bahrain? The only asset Bahrain has is oil! Do you need me to spell it out for you or do you get it? The U.S. only cares about a country when our corporations want something that country has. Young men and women risk their lives in fighting these wars so that corporations can get what they want and the CEOs can early millions while their employees earn a pittance.

I'm not sure what Hillary Clinton was referring to when she said there was a "vast right-wing conspiracy" but there definitely is one. Republicans do not want to fund Medicare and Social Security. They want to eliminate these programs and make everyone buy their own insurance and fund their own retirement. Why? Because the same Wall Street banksters, who brought you the financial meltdown where you saw your savings turned into penny stocks, want to get their hands on the money in the Social Security fund.

You need to realize what Republicans have done to our country. They stood by, after being warned by the Clinton administration that the terrorists were planning to fly planes into buildings, and allowed it to happen on 9/11. They started two wars (Iraq and Afghanistan) which cost us over a trillion dollars. They passed a Prescription Drug Benefit which provided the "benefit" to the pharmaceutical companies, not you. They bailed out the banks which cost us over $700 billion dollars and they turned around and foreclosed on your home.

To those who ask how long am I going to blame Republicans for the national debt and the financial collapse, the answer is FOREVER! They caused it. They own it. So, man up and accept responsibility for your failures Republicans. I know it is hard, baby, but you can do it!

If you expect our current politicians to fix everything for you, you are sadly mistaken. They make too much money with the present system to ever change it. You are going to have to run for office and make the changes. It won't happen quickly either because only so many senators are elected at a time. However, you could replace everyone in the House of Representatives in one election. Almost half of our Senators are over the age of sixty and most are in their seventies and eighties. How can they possibly be sharp enough and knowledgeable enough to handle the problems in the world today? I am over 70 and I wouldn't even think of running for office because I don't know how to deal with all the technology that we have today and that changes daily. We need young people in Congress.

GOVERNMENT 101

Based on the 2016 election, you clearly do not understand how government works so I am going to attempt to give you a brief education. In order to solve our problems, you need to understand just how government actually is supposed to work.

When most of you vote, you want instant gratification. You elected your representative in November and here it is January and they haven't fixed the nation's problems yet. But they haven't even taken office yet because they don't start until the end of January.

You elect a president every four years and they can only be re-elected once. The president, while limited by Congress, has many ways of changing the way government works. All he has to do is tell the departments under his control not to do something, as President George W. Bush did with the Securities and Exchange Commission. They were told not to enforce trading regulations. That is why you paid them to watch pornography eight hours a day instead of doing their job, which would have prevented the financial meltdown.

Here is the way federal elections work. Senators, of which there are 100 (two for each state) are elected for a 6-year term. Only one-third of the Senators are elected every two years. You can never do a full sweep of the Senate in one election. You may elect your party in one election but there is the possibility that the other two-thirds of the Senate will be made up of the other party. This is one reason why change doesn't happen instantly or at all.

The House of Representatives has 435 Representatives who are elected for a 2-year term. Every two years, they ALL come up for re-election. Representatives are allocated according to the population of a state. Each state does not have the same number of representatives. This is why it is so important that you complete your census form. The number of representatives you get is determined by the population. If you don't fill out the census, your state may lose a representative.

The House of Representatives has the sole power to originate revenue bills but they must be approved by the Senate. Here is where gridlock occurs because they can refuse to provide funds for programs and agencies they don't like thus stopping new laws or programs from being implemented. The House also has the sole power to bring charges of impeachment but those charges are referred to the Senate for a hearing. Evidence is presented in the Senate and not in the House as many people think. The Senate holds the trial with evidence and only the Senate can convict, and a two-thirds majority is necessary for a conviction.

The Senate has the sole power to approve Presidential appointments and treaties that the President may enter into with other countries.

For most bills, the Senate requires 60 votes for a bill to pass. However, there is a process called reconciliation where just a majority of votes are required but only to pass legislation that directly involves taxes and spending. Also, reconciliation legislation cannot be filibustered (a delay in voting when a senator speaks on the floor).

If you really want change, then you have to get over the idea that there can only be two parties - Democrats and Republicans. If you only have two teams, they will probably not cooperate. But if you have a third team, then they will have to cooperate.

One of the best senators for the human people is Bernie Sanders who was an Independent before he ran for president as a Democrat. It doesn't mean someone is crazy or not credible if they don't belong to one of the two parties. Had Bernie Sanders remained an Independent and ran as such, I am sure we would not have had the result of the 2016 election that we did.

While there are other parties on the ballots, they are limited to specific issues so therefore, they don't draw a lot of voters. The Independent Party is not what its name suggests. They believe in strict adherence to the Constitution and don't allow for any progressive changes.

After Trump destroyed the credibility of the Republican Party, we need a new party. We need a party that combines the best of both parties and reaches a common sense approach to solving our problems. Otherwise you have a constant tug-o-war and nothing gets done, which is what we have had for decades.

The other mindset that you need to change is voting based on name recognition. That is the worst reason to vote for someone. I have always believed that if we put Charlie Manson's name on the ballot, a lot of you would vote for him...some because you recognize the name and others because you like Charlie! You also vote for names that are easy to pronounce and spell. Not a good reason either. Many of you voted for George W. Bush because he looked like a guy you'd want to have a beer with! You saw how well that philosophy worked.

In reality, establishing a credible third party would solve a lot of our problems because the Democrats and Republicans would be forced to work with other members instead of having a majority and telling the party not in the majority that they are irrelevant, as was done in previous elections.

Another reason to have a third party is that currently if you don't like the person running in your party, it is very difficult for someone new to secure the support of the party if the party likes the current candidate. This was proven by Bernie Sanders trying to run against Hillary Clinton. The party was committed to her and brought out their super delegates to give her the win.

FEDERAL GOVERNMENT

BRANCH	DUTIES	TERM OF OFFICE
Executive Branch President Carries out Laws	**Checks on the Legislative and Judicial Branches** Can propose laws Can veto laws Makes Appointments Negotiates foreign treaties Appoint Federal Judges Grant pardons to federal prisoners	4 Years with 2 term limit
Legislative Branch **Senate** 100 Senators (2 from each State)	**Checks on the Executive and Judicial Branches** *Pass Legislation *Override a Presidential veto *Initiate constitutional amendments *Declare war *Confirm a newly appointed Vice-President Confirm Appointments Ratify treaties Try cases of Impeachment Elect Vice-Pesident if Electoral College is tied	6 Year term with I/3 elected every 2 years
House of Representatives 435 Representatives	*Pass Legislation *Override a Presidential veto *Initiate constitutional amendments *Declare war *Confirm a newly appointed Vice-President Initiate spending bills Bring impeachment charges Elect Pesident if Electoral College is tied * These are shared powers. Presidential Veto and impeachment must have a 2/3 majority in both chambers	2 Year Term
Judicial Branch 9 Justices	**Checks on the Executive and Legislative Branches** Can declare executive actions and laws unconstitutional	Lifetime Appointment

Figure 1FEDERAL GOVERNMENT

HOW DOES A **BILL** BECOME A **LAW?**

1 EVERY LAW STARTS WITH AN IDEA

That idea can come from anyone, even you! Contact your elected officials to share your idea. If they want to try to make it a law, they will write a bill.

2 THE BILL IS INTRODUCED

A bill can start in either house of Congress when it's introduced by its primary sponsor, a Senator or a Representative. In the House of Representatives, bills are placed in a wooden box called "the hopper."

Here, the bill is assigned a legislative number before the Speaker of the House sends it to a committee.

3 THE BILL GOES TO COMMITTEE

Representatives or Senators meet in a small group to research, talk about, and make changes to the bill. They vote to accept or reject the bill and its changes before sending it to:

the House or Senate floor for debate or **to a subcommittee for further research.**

4 CONGRESS DEBATES AND VOTES

Members of the House or Senate can now debate the bill and propose changes or amendments before voting. If the majority vote for and pass the bill, it moves to the other house to go through a similar process of committees, debate, and voting. Both houses have to agree on the same version of the final bill before it goes to the President.

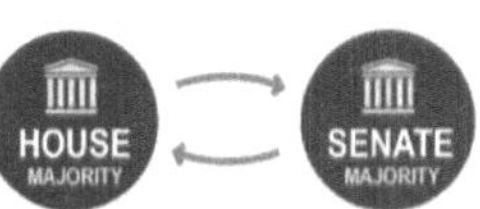

DID YOU KNOW?

The House uses an electronic voting system while the Senate typically votes by voice, saying "yay" or "nay."

5 PRESIDENTIAL ACTION

When the bill reaches the President, he or she can:

✓ APPROVE and PASS

The President signs and approves the bill. The bill is law.

THE BILL IS **LAW**

The President can also:

Veto

The President rejects the bill and returns it to Congress with the reasons for the veto. Congress can override the veto with 2/3 vote of those present in both the House and the Senate and the bill will become law.

Choose no action

The President can decide to do nothing. If Congress is in session, after 10 days of no answer from the President, the bill then automatically becomes law.

Pocket veto

If Congress adjourns (goes out of session) within the 10 day period after giving the President the bill, the President can choose not to sign it and the bill will not become law.

Brought to you by 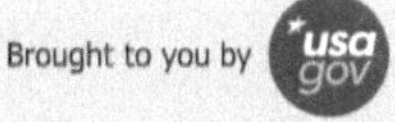 usa gov

Figure 2HOW A BILL BECOMES A LAW

For a bill to become a law, it requires a majority of both houses and the president's signature. If it fails in either step, it can't become a law. This is why it is important for you to give the president a Congress that doesn't oppose the president along party lines. If you give a Republican president a Democratic Congress or vice versa, probably not much will get done. Don't blame the person you voted for, blame yourself.

In an ideal world, everyone would cooperate for the good of the country. But this isn't the ideal world, and our system is run by people who only look out for their own good. You have to not just vote for president but for a Congress (senators and representatives) who will support the president. Until such time as a viable third party emerges, you will have to vote this way. Once you have a viable third party, then that will force the other two parties to compromise and work to fix our problems. Until such time, it will be like a game of tug-o-war. The right pulls one way and the left the other way.

ABORTION

There isn't an issue that riles up Republicans more than abortion. They supposedly care about unborn children. But where the hell are they after the child is born and put in a trash bag and dumped in a trash bin like yesterday's burger? Where are they when the child is beaten repeatedly by their parents until it is finally murdered?

I don't think there is anyone that really likes abortion but there are times when it is necessary. A child or woman is raped. But there are also other times when you may not like it but, to that person, it is necessary. They stupidly had sex and got pregnant and have no means to support the baby. I know they can always give it up for adoption, but often they don't and it ends up beaten to death or flushed down a toilet.

This is just me, but I would rather have the child aborted before it is born and thinks it will have a good life and then is beaten to death or constantly abused. How many of these Bible waving pro-life people actually step up to the plate and adopt some of these children? How many have ever protested when a parent is charged with murdering the child? I have never seen any pro-lifers at the trials of these murderers.

SOLUTION

Both sides need to agree on a certain time when abortion is no longer permitted. There is ample time from the moment a woman realizes that she is pregnant to abort the baby.

But more important, part of the solution should be to educate men and women about sexual behavior. You will have the drug addicts who have sex for drugs and get pregnant. No amount of education is going to stop that. There was a drug addict in Orange County, California who had several babies and this one couple always adopted them. Finally, the people adopting the babies, offered to pay for the woman to have a hysterectomy but the ACLU opposed that. So, the woman had the right to keep popping drug addicted babies out like a PEZ dispenser and the ACLU was ok with that?

Women should also be allowed to obtain birth control pills from any facility. If you are going to allow men to get Viagra which keeps their sex drive going, then you need to allow women to obtain birth control pills. If you are a religious facility acting as a corporation, then you must abide by the same rules. Sell the pills or go out of business. No exceptions!

ARBITRATION

There is hardly anything you do anymore that doesn't require you to sign an arbitration clause that waives your right to sue a company in a court of law. I ordered a roll of Alien tape and in the box was an arbitration agreement! The Church of Scientology requires members to sign arbitration agreements whereby they will not sue the church for anything that happens to them including rape. This was another inept decision by the Supreme Court.

First of all, you are giving up your right to trial by jury, something guaranteed by the Constitution. The companies requiring you to sign, say you have the right to refuse. But they don't say that if you refuse, in most cases, you can't get the service or product you want because they require you to waive that right. Take it or leave it is hardly a choice, especially when you are dealing with a bank or utility company. In many cases, you don't have a choice to go somewhere else for the service. If they all stick together, you are screwed.

Corporations prefer arbitration because it prevents you from joining a class action legal suit. Corporations know that most attorneys will not take an action by just one claimant. They prefer to lump them into a class action so that they don't have to try each case individually.

This is most beneficial when a company manufactures a product that causes cancer in many people. To sue on behalf of each person would be cost prohibitive. In a class action lawsuit, all cases are combined and any award is split among all the claimants.

SOLUTION

Simple. Arbitration should be banned unless the person can still get the service or product without agreeing to arbitration.

CAMPAIGN FINANCING

Our politicians spend more time raising money for their next campaign than they do working on our nation's problems. They earn under $200,000 a year, yet many of them and their families are now millionaires. They weren't millionaires when they took office. How do you turn $200,000 into a million if you aren't accepting bribes from someone who wants you to vote a certain way on a piece of legislation?

Some refer to politicians as whores, but that is an insult to whores everywhere. With a whore, you know exactly what you are going to get and what it is going to cost. The same cannot be said of a politician.

Former House Speaker Dennis Hastert is a good example of this. When he took office his net worth was no more than $290,000. During his 19-year tenure, he managed to increase his net worth to over $6 million. When hurricane Katrina hit, Speaker Hastert couldn't return to Washington to deal with the destruction because he had to attend a fund raiser!

Our politicians have set up all kinds of non-profits to hide their contributions. If they don't take money outright, they hide it by employing family members in their non-profits. Thrown into the mix are PACS (Political Action Committees), where more money can be contributed for expenses. Donald Trump continues to raise money even though he lost the election and he can use this money for anything he wants – his family, his golf trips, and his haircuts.

The money spent on political campaigns and initiatives is passed on to you and I because we pay more for the products and services the corporations provide to the government.

SOLUTION:

1. The media, as part of their FCC licenses should provide time for debates among the top candidates for office. Newspapers can provide a candidate's statement in an election supplement. We don't need a barrage of sleezy TV ads that run years in advance of an election.

    The debate for president should cover issues that the country faces at the time and not the silly questions asked by most so-called journalists. The people should decide based on the solutions the candidates offer and not a bunch of lies and accusations or whether the candidate wears briefs or boxers (as one journalist asked of Bill Clinton.)

2. Local TV stations should provide time for debates among the representatives for the Senate and House of Representatives. If this is the only way they can reach the people, then they will have to get more serious about their campaigns and won't be wasting their time talking about their opponent's sex life or their religion.

3. LIMIT CAMPAIGN PERIOD - The campaign period should be no longer than six months before an election. This will keep the incumbents in Washington where they belong and not off campaigning for a year or two before the election.

4. QUALIFICATIONS FOR OFFICE - First of all, no one with a felony conviction should hold public office. Currently, is up to the House or Senate to decide if someone convicted of a felony may serve in Congress. Local politicians often

make deals with judges, if convicted of a felony, to have their record expunged if they comply with certain restrictions. Try that with YOUR judge if, God forbid, you are ever convicted of a felony and see how far you get. It didn't work for Martha Stewart!

In most states, a convicted felon is prohibited from voting. Yet a convicted felon is permitted to vote in Congress! Has your head exploded yet? Why do we have such a law? Because our legislators wrote it to protect their own deplorables. Also, members of Congress cannot be tried for insider trading. How nice that they exempted themselves from that.

IMPACT:

This will end the practice of politicians being paid off by corporations. Only politicians who truly care about the country will run for office.

WHO WILL OPPOSE IT:

The politicians who now come into office owning nothing and leave millionaires will definitely oppose this legislation. They will scream that it is a violation of their and their corporate people's free speech. You know what crybabies they are. Just look at former Ohio Representative John Boehner who once passed out checks from the tobacco industry on the floor of Congress! Yes, your representatives won't like this legislation, so get out the Kleenex because they will cry up a storm!

CORRUPTION

It should come as no surprise that corruption is the number one problem because it began with our very first president. After losing his first election to the Virginia House of Burgesses because he didn't buy drinks for the voters, George Washington learned. The next election, his aide made sure there was spiked punch and George Washington won. The problem still exists. Only instead of spiked punch, big contributors to our legislators now demand their votes in exchange for money or jobs for family members.

A lobbyist who had given money to Teddy Roosevelt's campaign later said, when Roosevelt didn't vote the way they wanted him to, "we bought that son of a bitch but he wouldn't stay bought."

If we don't stop corruption in all levels of government, we will never be able to afford to solve our other problems.

The dumbest statement ever made was by a resident of Carson, California. Mayor Daryl Sweeney was convicted of corruption involving millions of dollars in municipal contracts. This resident wrote in the newspaper that "It wasn't like he took our money!"

If you are like this Carson resident and don't think that government employees taking bribes from contractors will increase the cost of the contract, you are naive. Do you honestly think a contractor would just give someone millions of dollars without adding it to the cost of the contract? This is why our public officials are always wanting to increase our taxes.

In 2002 lobbyists paid over $1.5 billion dollars to our Congressmen and Congresswomen. That is $1.5 billion that should have gone to shareholders of those corporations. In addition to the greed at the federal level of our government, you also have the state, county and city employees taking bribes as well.

Politicians don't like to call it a bribe. But whether you call it a campaign contribution, a donation to the politician's own charity, or a job for a relative, it is still a bribe. No corporation is going to give a politician that kind of money unless they get something in return. This is why almost all politicians have their own charities. They will never say, "Oh donate the money to the Red Cross or to cancer research. Most of their own charities have relatives in charge drawing a salary (i.e. the Clinton Foundation).

Whether it is the city inspector who takes $100 to approve your permit or your Senator who takes millions to approve legislation, the bottom line is YOU pay for it. You pay for it in taxes which pay for the contracts and you pay for it in lost earnings on your investments in those corporations.

This is also why things don't get fixed properly. For example, if the building had a leaky roof, rather than repair the roof, the politician's solution would be to give everyone a bucket because they have a campaign contributor who sells buckets.

THE SOLUTION: A simple law that states the following:

No government employee or candidate for office or their immediate family members (defined as spouses, parents, and children, natural or adopted) may take anything from any lobbyist, corporation or its employees who are A) Seeking to do any business with the government over which that government employee or candidate will have any control and B) Seeking the employee's or candidate's support for legislation which will be of benefit to said lobbyist, corporation or employee thereof. If it is later found that said government employee or family member did take anything, then that contract or legislation will be voided and the employee will be immediately fired with loss of retirement benefits and the corporation and its officers banned for ten years from bidding on any other government contracts. This ban also applies to non-profit corporations under the ownership or control of any government employee or their immediate family members as defined above, who receive any compensation or benefit from said non-profit corporation.

As a condition of employment as a government employee, said employee and the above- named family members must submit a yearly statement of all of their assets. This is to flag illegal payments to government employees or their immediate family members.

IMPACT:

1. This law will stop corporations from buying politicians and other government employees.

2. This law will reduce the cost of government programs because corporations won't have to pay bribes to government employees and can reduce the cost of the products or services they seek to provide to the government. The military is the largest government agency that will benefit from this law. Perhaps then, Cher won't have to buy helmet inserts for soldiers because the military will be able to ensure that the soldiers receive the proper equipment before sending them into war.

WHO WILL OPPOSE THIS LAW?

First, of course, those government employees who are currently taking bribes or donations (wink, wink) will oppose it. While corporations would ultimately benefit financially by not having to pay lobbyists, they will probably oppose the law because while it costs them money, they also reap huge bloated contracts for their corporations.

HOW DO WE DO THIS WHEN CONGRESS
WON'T PROPOSE SUCH LEGISLATION?

It will have to be done on a state by state basis through initiatives because we know it will never get anywhere with our current representatives. This is like asking the wolf to watch the chickens when you go on vacation.

But the problem here is that only a few states have the initiative process available. So, if your state does not have the initiative process available, then YOU must run for office and throw out the current bunch of corrupt politicians.

President Obama said it best in his farewell speech to the nation when he said, "So, you see, that's what our democracy demands. It needs you. Not just when there's an election, not just when your own narrow interest is at stake, but over the full span of a lifetime. If you're tired of arguing with strangers on the Internet, try talking with one of them in real life. If something needs fixing, then lace up your shoes and do some organizing. If you're disappointed by your elected officials, grab the clipboard, get some signatures, AND RUN FOR OFFICE YOURSELF. Show up. Dive in. Stay at it."

The prior attempts on a federal level to regulate campaign contributions made things worse because they allowed the creation of non-profits to shield donors and allow unlimited money to be given to legislators through super pacs (Political Action Committees).

The Supreme Court ruled in Citizens United that corporations are "people" and can contribute unlimited funds to politicians. But YOU have proven time and time again that money doesn't matter when citizens UNITE. Mitt Romney, Carly Fiorina, Meg Whitman and numerous other would- be politicians lost their presidential bid because the CITIZENS UNITED and voted for the other candidate. Money doesn't speak when you get out and vote. But it does speak when you don't vote.

If you don't do one other thing, you must pass legislation as I have written it to stop corruption. Do not expect our current politicians to do so because they are making too much money through corruption. If you don't do this, then forget about fixing anything else because any solutions will be tied to some politician getting money for voting for a specific solution.

DEATH PENALTY

People have the mistaken idea that the death penalty is supposed to be a deterrent. The fear of the death penalty is supposed to make someone stop from committing murder. This is wrong for two reasons. First of all, it was to deter THAT particular person, and not others. Secondly everyone knows that the death penalty is not enforced anymore so how can it possibly be a deterrent.

Let me give you an example of where a law not enforced is not a deterrent. When I bought a condo, it was discovered that someone had gained access to it and had been living in it unbeknownst to the owner. I changed the locks and while I was putting things away, I found someone's belongings in the master bedroom along with their ID. I called the police and they came and picked up the belongings. Then someone rang the doorbell and it was the person who had been living there. Seems the realtor gave him the code to the lock box and he got the key, duplicated it, and had a place to live for free. He wanted to know where his stuff was and I told him the police had it. So, he says "Well, I know they'll lock me up for a couple days but at least I'll get my stuff back." He knew he would not be locked up for very long.

When a person knows that very little, if anything, will happen to them in the way of a punishment, they do it!

If you buy a bag of apples and one is rotten, do you leave it in the bag hoping that it will miraculously not be rotten? Of course not. It is ridiculous to hope that a drug dealer will change when murder is the way they enforce their rules. Many of the convicted murderers have gone on to murder people in prison. The only way to stop them is to execute them. Whether a person will change or not depends on the circumstances of the murder.

SOLUTION

While I agree that a person should have a proper trial, I also acknowledge that in some areas of the country, a person will not get a fair trial due to the bias of the officer, the district attorney, the judge, or the jury. In those cases, I think the death penalty should not be an option. Until such time as we rid our judicial system of prejudice, we need to hold back on the death penalty.

But in cases where there is no doubt whatsoever and a person is caught in the act with witnesses or on camera, then go for it!

 SHIRLEY CONLEY

THE ECONOMY

There is an Amish saying that says, "He who has little and wants less is richer than he who has much and wants more." The economy collapsed because of corporate greed. CEOs, once the economy had collapsed, decided that they could do without a lot of employees by making the ones they kept do the work of two people. Instead of taking the profits and putting them back into the corporation, the CEOs increased their own salaries.

CEOs currently earn over 400 times what the average employee earns. Many of these CEOs earn exorbitant salaries while their corporations lose money. Wall Street employees who caused the meltdown were rewarded with bonuses! Then these same people bought up your houses that went into foreclosure and made money from you once again when they sold them back to you or someone else.

Henry Ford understood in 1914 that "profit sharing" was the best way to run a corporation. He paid his employees $5.00 per day ($110 today) which upset other corporations. But Ford wanted his workers to be able to afford the cars that they manufactured. As a result, he was able to hire the best mechanics in the industry, thus reducing his training costs. He raised productivity because employees who had a share of the profits worked harder and didn't steal from the company.

Since 1978, CEO wages have increased by 940% while the workers, who do the actual work, only saw an 11.9% increase in their wages.

The corporations today will not add jobs nor share their profits with their employees. They got their wish in 2016 thanks to YOU because YOU gave Republicans control of the Presidency, the Senate, the House of Representatives, many state Governorships, and now control of the U.S. Supreme Court. You took away control of the House of Representatives in 2018 but then gave Republicans overwhelming control of the Senate. What the hell were you thinking?

We are no longer a democracy but rather a corporatocracy - a government run by corporations. Remember corporations love to privatize the profits and socialize the losses (that means YOU the human person pays when the corporate person loses money.)

When the United States was founded, the only source of income was tariffs charged on foreign products from Europe. It wasn't until August 5, 1861 that the income tax came into being as a result of the American Civil War. Up until the war, we got along fine by taxing foreign products.

One of the worst things that happened to our country was NAFTA (North American Free Trade Agreement) signed by President Bill Clinton. Once this agreement went into effect, corporations started closing U.S. plants and moving to countries that had cheap labor and little regulation. Those jobs, mostly for working class people, are not coming back. No one, Bill Clinton included, cared about what was going to happen to the people who lost their jobs. Oh yes, NAFTA created jobs - just not in our country.

Corporations have made us afraid to speak out against them by threatening to leave the country if we don't cut taxes and regulations. They are like the abusive spouse who belittles the other spouse into thinking they can't survive without them. Well, guess what? We, the human people, are some of the top consumers of merchandise and services in the world. If WE stop spending, guess what happens to the corporate profits? If corporations want to move their plants off shore, let them. But their products can't come back into the country until they pay the tariffs. This is one point in particular where I agreed with Donald Trump.

THE SOLUTION:

1. The government should rescind those free trade agreements or at the very least, change the removal of tariffs on products.

2. The government should arrange for the employees of plants that moved out of the U.S. to receive loans that will allow them to reopen those plants and start producing products again in this country. This will put skilled people back to work. There won't be a need for unions because the employees will control the company. Productivity will increase because employees will know that they will receive part of the profits if the company does well. This will increase income for people and the government. CEO salaries should be limited to that of the President of the United States, plus profit-sharing. No profits - no sharing! Oh, and profit sharing will be for all employees, not just management.

3. We need to train people in jobs that will be needed in the future.

4. We need to end tax credits given to corporations to move their jobs overseas. Why we did this in the first place is beyond logic.

5. We need to place caps on executive pay. This will be explained in the Investors Assurance Act in another chapter.

IMPACT:

Jobs will return to the U.S.

Tariffs will provide income to run the government and that will mean less taxes that you and I have to pay.

CEOs will now have to prove their worth. They will no longer receive millions for running their corporations into bankruptcy.

The U.S. will once again become a producer of quality products because the employees will have a reason to care about the corporation.

WHO WILL OPPOSE THIS?

Obviously corporate CEOs earning exorbitant salaries will not like this. One of the basic rules for investing is "Leave something for someone else." CEOs need to leave some money for other employees. You know—the ones who actually do the work!

A case in point is Warner Music Group Corporation's CEO Edgar Bronfman who earned $3.42 million after Warner lost $21 million and shares of Warner fell 68%. Talk about rewarding incompetence! How can that possibly be justified? The corporate mantra was "We have to pay CEOs high salaries so that we can get qualified people." I am sure there is someone in India who would be willing to run Warner for a lot less compensation and probably do a much better job.

The countries benefiting from the free trade agreement will not be in favor of rescinding the agreement, but there has to be a balance somewhere. Our representatives must protect we, the HUMAN PEOPLE from we, the CORPORATE PEOPLE.

EDUCATION

The No Child Left Behind Act required all children to pass certain tests and penalized those schools whose students failed to pass the tests. There is one major problem with that piece of legislation. Not all schools are created equal. The student in Beverly Hills has the latest computers, books, and quality teachers. The child in Compton, California often has to share books, use donated computers if they even have any, and has to worry when it rains if the roof will leak on their classroom.

A major problem is that education is funded by taxes on the homes in the area of the school. Any idiot can figure out that the taxes paid on a home in Compton are much less than a home in Beverly Hills. Hence, the money available to the schools is also different.

Only when schools have equal access to learning materials, equipment and quality teachers, can the testing standard be fair. Why hasn't anyone in Congress figured this out in hundreds of years?

SOLUTION:

A. STANDARD GUIDELINE FOR BASICS

Every child needs the same quality of education. There are three subjects that should be standard no matter where you live - reading, math, and computer skills. We need to find the Jamie Escalantes* in teaching and have them develop a teaching plan for those subjects. Then all teachers across the country must follow those programs.

With a set teaching plan, then you can evaluate students and teachers fairly. If teachers want to be creative, let them teach art, writing, government, civics or sports. But the basic knowledge that all students need, should be set in stone because that doesn't change.

B. EDUCATION FUNDING

Either we pool school tax funds so that all schools, regardless of where they are located have the same books and equipment or the federal government picks up the tab. But we need to equalize the playing field. It is ridiculous that parents have to decide where to live based on the quality of the schools in a given area. All schools should have the same quality of education. You shouldn't have to drive your child to school in another area because the schools there are better than the schools where you live. Also, teachers should not be spending their own money on supplies. What other job would make you buy what you need to do your job?

C. INTERNET INTERFACE

This next part was written before the pandemic so I was way ahead of the game.

---

* Jamie Escalante was a math teacher from Garfield High School in East Los Angeles who taught students who were considered "unteachable and troubled" calculus. Most of these "unteachables" went on to pass the Advanced Placement Calculus Test.

We are a mobile society. Many parents have to move to a new area due to their jobs, which mean that their children are taken out of school and thrust into a new school in a new area with new teachers and new friends. This is another reason for standardized lesson plans so that if you move from New York to California, your child doesn't suddenly find himself or herself ahead of or behind the rest of the class at the new school. If it's Tuesday, they are on Lesson 6 in New York and in California.

Almost every home has a computer and those that don't should be given an affordable one for their child to use for school work. If you don't like the idea of giving students computers, (Los Angeles Unified School District had a failed program when they gave computers to students to take home and back to school with them) then set up a TV instruction program where the day's lessons are broadcast free on demand. That way, if a child is sick or can't attend school, they can get their lesson on TV at home.

As a parent, if your child is being educated from home, you need to establish a separate area for them to use the computer where they will be uninterrupted so they can concentrate.

D. ENGLISH IMMERSION CLASSES

To prove that we the people have better ideas than Congress, Judy Winick of Los Angeles stated in an editorial that "Immersion in our language should be the first priority for non-English speakers."

We are a nation of immigrants. Get over it. It's a fact. This is our reality. We need to set up English immersion classes so that before children enter public schools, they can speak English well enough to understand the classes. I can't imagine sitting in a classroom where I had no idea what was being said. Yet we ask children to do this every day. Then we fault teachers because these students are failing.

Let me give you an example of what it would be like sitting in a class where you don't understand what is being taught. After chemotherapy, I was left totally deaf in my left ear and a large hearing loss in my right ear. Even though I watch TV with the closed captioning on, there are many times that I don't know what is being said. If the people speak very fast, then the people in India doing the closed captioning can't keep up so I end up missing a lot of what is being said. Not being able to understand what is being taught is the same as being deaf.

This will eliminate the need for bilingual teachers in subjects other than the English immersion classes.

E. MENTOR PROGRAM

I cringed every time I heard President Obama say to parents, "Spend time with your kids. Read to them." I guess President Obama never knew what it was like to have parents who can't read or write, or who do not speak English. His parents were both well-educated and he had someone to help him with his homework. But there are thousands of children out there whose parents can't read or write, so how are they going to sit down and help them read?

The biggest mistake people make is using their own experience to decide what others want or need. Obama assumed that all families were able to help their children with their homework. That simply is not a reality. People may be well educated but not educated in the reality of others.

Schools need to develop a mentoring program with local colleges whereby the college students, for credit, help those students whose parents are unable to help them. Even high school students, juniors or seniors, could participate in the program to assist children in the lower grades. Some schools already have such programs, but every school should have such a program.

F. STUDENT EVALUATION

Students should be evaluated for their interests and their skills. Not all students will go to college. Some will become sports players, artists, musicians, or mechanics. There is no need to subject them to college prep classes when they will never attend college and may drop out of school due to the degree of difficulty of college prep classes.

This is why it is so important to have arts classes in schools. Music and art are just as necessary as reading and math. Look at all the actors and actresses and musicians who have successful careers without ever going to college.

Place students in classes that will not only educate them in their area of interest, but will stimulate their desire to learn. Offer classes in home construction, mechanics, or computer repair.

G. BASIC ACCOUNTING

I can't stress enough the need to provide a basic course in accounting. It is not too early to start in late elementary school or middle school. It can be a fun project by having the students pick a business they would like to start and guide them in how to establish it and find out if they made money or lost money.

This will prepare the students for managing their finances later in life. Many small businesses fail because the owners were ignorant about basic accounting. They know the product but don't know how to calculate what it costs to produce that product and all the other costs related to getting it to market.

Just look at the actors and sports figures who have lost all their earnings to unscrupulous managers. At least if a person can understand the basic principles of accounting, they will be able to monitor their finances. Simply saying, "I can always hire someone to handle my finances" is foolish. If you don't know how to read a financial statement, then you are setting yourself up for failure.

GOVERNMENT STUDIES

The fact that so many people do not understand how government works, just proves that our teachers are not teaching. John Wynne said "Schools need to be the incubator where future voters are taught the skills needed to participate in our complex society." The most important thing you will ever do to preserve our democratic way of life, is vote and yet most of you don't understand how your government operates.

A government class should be exciting and encourage the student to want to participate in the process. Yet when I took Government in school, my biggest challenge was to stay awake. There was nothing that made me want to get involved. Part of the class should be a mandatory volunteer stint in an election process. Work the polls or work on a campaign.

BENEFITS OF THE PLAN:

1. When children move to another city, they won't be left behind anymore.

2. Standard lesson plans and equal equipment will place children on equal footing in exit exams.

3. Children will be less apt to drop out of school and society will benefit by having a better educated population.

4. Any time a society seeks to educate its people, everyone benefits. Ignorance is NOT bliss.

WHO WILL OPPOSE THIS PLAN?

Teachers who think their way is the best way, yet their students fail to graduate. This is not to say teachers can't introduce better ways to teach. They can. It is just that they have a certain lesson plan that they have to teach on schedule. People hoping to get government money to start a private or charter school who are in it for the money only and not for the students will oppose the plan.

ENVIRONMENT

Once again, the same corporate people that President Lincoln spoke of are calling environmentalists alarmists and have convinced some of you that there is no such thing as global warming. After all, it snowed! They are the masters of public relations and can convince you to believe them over believing your eyes. The mistake scientists made was calling it global warming although parts of the world are melting and disappearing. They should have called it corporate pollution which is causing cancer and other health diseases. That is a name we can all relate to. But when we are freezing, it is hard to believe in global warming. That was just an unfortunate name for a real condition. But then well-educated people have trouble communicating on a level that others can understand and thus leave themselves vulnerable to propaganda by the opposing side.

All you have to do is look at a photo of the polar ice caps taken at different times and you can see that they are melting. As the ice melts, it throws more water into the oceans and into the atmosphere. That increases the rainfall and the strength of the oceans.

I guess if there is any consolation in this debate it is this. The increase of water and the severity of the storms will impact the lands along the oceans, which are usually occupied by the same wealthy people who oppose global warming. So eventually their property will be destroyed by that which they deny exists.

Why do you think the wealthy are in such a hurry to find life on another planet and are lining up and putting money down on space trips to other places? Because they know they have destroyed this planet and want to get the hell out of here before it all blows. Who do you think will be able to afford a space flight elsewhere? Let me give you a hint – NOT YOU! You will never be able to afford it so you will have to stay here on planet earth and eat contaminated food and look for drinkable water

We have seen the result of deregulation with the nuclear meltdown in Japan from the tsunami. The fact is that while nuclear energy may not pollute the air while operating properly, it produces toxic waste that we simply cannot get rid of for thousands of years, if ever. We have no safe place to store it. Here's an idea. When the wealthy leave for another planet, mandate that they have to take drums of nuclear waste with them.

Environmentalists are not very well organized but tend to be henny penny in their issues. They raised a fuss over plastic grocery bags claiming they were single use. But they were not single use. Many of us used them under the sink for trash. We used them to pick up after our dogs. We used them to put our lunch in when we went to work. If they wanted to get rid of any grocery bags, they should have gotten rid of the produce bags because they are totally single use and just barely useful for their intended purpose. Did you ever try to get them open to put your carrots in? You have to struggle to get them open and usually they tear before you succeed. If they make it home, they serve no other purpose. They missed the boat on this issue. The replacement bags can eventually spread disease if not cleaned after putting meat in them. Some are made from polypropylene which causes cancer. Since the pandemic, we can't bring our own bags, so these polypropylene bags are going to go into the landfills.

The other thing they banned was plastic straws for your drinks but they have done nothing about plastic water bottles or other liquid bottles. I was complaining to a clerk at Target about the ban on plastic bags and remarked that they should ban plastic water bottles which I see everywhere and when I looked down into the large part of my cart, I saw a used water bottle. I looked at the clerk and said "I rest my case."

Another thing I have not heard anyone address is all the junk we are putting into space. There are corporations sending junk into space every day and what will happen to all that? Has ANYONE in our government (certainly not the 80- year old politicians who probably don't even know it is up there) ever thought about what is going to happen to all that junk? Maybe some of it will burn up but the rest may just come crashing down on your house the way waste from airplanes does when they empty a toilet in space. I haven't heard environmentalists mention this.

PRODUCTS FROM CHINA

I am absolutely astounded that the environmentalists have said NOTHING about all the crap made in China that goes into our landfills every day! Here are just a couple examples that I personally have encountered and I am sure you have many more products from China that you had to throw in the trash.

I purchased potholders that were made in China. What is the purpose of a potholder? To protect your hand from heat when you reach to get something out of the oven. The very first time I used this potholder, when I reached to grab a dish out of the oven, the potholder melted! Yes melted! And then I have to deal with the mess of whatever it was made of that stuck to my oven rack.

I also purchased outdoor solar lights that were made in China. Solar means they get their energy from the sun. Whatever they were made of disintegrated from the sun. One day I saw the light on the ground and went to put it back on the metal post when I saw that the whole top of it had crumbled from exposure to the sun.

Everyone knows that if you want quality engineering you go to Germany or Switzerland. If you want style and quality sewing, you go to France or Italy. And if you want cheap crap you go to China.

Think about it. What are you really saving when you buy something cheap from China and it only last a few weeks and then you have to buy it all over again? Wouldn't it be better to pay a little more for it and buy something made in the U.S.A. – if they still manufactured things here? If you have to buy a $10 item four times a year that would be $40. But if a U.S.A. product sells for $30, you would be ahead $10 and still have a working product and our landfills would not be filled with this crap from China.

I still have a Waring blender that was made in the U.S.A. that I got as a wedding present over 50 years ago and it still works perfectly. In fact, it has lasted 45 years longer than the marriage. However, I have a Shark iron that I bought a few months ago, that will end up in the trash because it never gets hot enough to iron.

Whatever you put into your trash can ends up in a landfill and eventually whatever these products were made of will seep into our water supply. This is a hell of a lot more serious than the plastic straws or plastic grocery bags. You didn't do well with the shortage of toilet paper during the pandemic but imagine NO WATER to drink! Yet the environmentalists are totally silent on this serious issue. Trust me. This is a real problem.

Corporations for years have polluted water and land and gotten away with it and then you and I have to pay to clean up their mess. A good example of this is, which I have mentioned earlier, is the Exide battery plant in California that for years dumped their waste into the ground. All the people in the area are getting cancer. Exide paid a pittance toward cleaning up the area and it is far from cleaned up. California is on the hook for billions of dollars to clean it up. That means you and I are going to pay – not Exide. Exide PRIVATIZED THEIR PROFITS AND SOCIALIZED THEIR LOSSES!

ELECTRIC VEHICLES

Many of the governors are pushing to have only electric cars available in ten to fifteen years. However, I don't hear one of them, in their proposals, state where the electricity is going to come from. They also do not mention what they are going to do with the batteries when they die. From our experience with Exide, we know what an environmental hazard batteries can be, yet they make no mention of this.

Some are relying on solar and wind for energy. But are they taking into account what may happen to solar and wind if the climate starts changing and the sun is snubbed out or the winds change? Do we end up creating a worse environmental disaster while trying to solve another one? If Exide was able to cause that much damage with the small car batteries used to start the car, imagine what they can do with the huge batteries that power the cars.

SOLUTION TO ENVIRONMENT

Here's a thought. Since we are going to have so much more water in the oceans, why not use hydroelectric power? Just as soon as one of the corporations comes up with a way to OWN the water in the ocean, it will happen.

We are already turning to solar and wind power which is clean and inexpensive. This is a step in the right direction but the scientists need to evaluate what impact changes in the environment will will have on these solutions.

We do NOT need deregulation. We already have seen what happens when corporations are left to regulate themselves. They simply don't.

Corporations must take out a bond to cover clean-up costs before they can start a project. The bond must cover the total cost of clean-up in a worse-case scenario.

WHO WILL OPPOSE IT

The same greedy corporations that gave us $5.00 a gallon gasoline while taking billions of our dollars over the years in subsidies will not like a plan that makes them RESPONSIBLE. But if they are truly worth their obscene salaries then they will take their corporation in a direction that we the human people want to go. But expect deadly resistance from the oil, coal, and nuclear industries. They will stop at nothing to protect their own self interests. They could care less about the environment.

Here is the bottom line on the environmental issue. If the environmentalists are wrong, there is no harm done. Corporations will just have to spend more money on cleaning up their waste. But if the environmentalists are right and you do nothing, the damage will be irreversible. Just look at the damage the oil spill in the Gulf of Mexico caused. Wildlife and sea creatures were destroyed. Jobs were lost because of oil washing up on the beaches. Was it worth the deregulation of the oil industry? How many times are you willing to get cancer?

Republicans went on TV and blasted President Obama because he held British Petroleum RESPONSIBLE for the spill and made them place billions of dollars in a fund to reimburse human people who were injured, lost their jobs as a result of the spill, or suffered other monetary damage. Had President Obama not taken this step, human people would have had to wait years to settle with BP.

★ ★ ★ ★ ★

FAIRNESS DOCTRINE

The Fairness Doctrine established in 1949 stated that the broadcast media must present both sides of a controversial issue of public importance in an honest and balanced manner. However, in 1987 the Federal Communications Commission, under President Ronald Reagan, removed the language that implemented the Doctrine. The Fairness Doctrine is not the same as the "equal time" rule which pertains only to candidates, not issues. Equal time means that if you have one candidate on your show, you must give the opposing candidate equal time to appear at a later date. This does not apply to political advertising.

President Obama opposed efforts to reinstate the Fairness Doctrine and thought that by limiting the ownership of media networks, it would provide fairness. It did not. For example, Fox News only presents one point of view on its cable network. I find it rather amusing that even Osama Bin Laden recognized that Fox News was a biased station, yet millions of you don't. Most stations will report the news and not give their own opinion. There are other shows that are only opinion shows and not news shows (i.e. Fox). They merely present one side of the story. Let me clarify something here. There is Fox Cable News, which is opinion news. Then there is your local access Fox station which usually does NOT do opinion news.

The easiest way to determine if the station you listen to or watch presents both sides of an issue, just call them and present an opposing point of view and see if they put you on the air. If they repeatedly present only their side of an issue, then TURN THEM OFF! You will never hear the truth from them. Also, do they ever issue a statement saying that they reported something in error? If they don't, TURN THEM OFF!

Here are just two of many websites where you can fact check something that is being said. One is snope.com and the other is FactCheckd.org.

It used to be that there were both conservative and progressive radio stations to listen to. There was Randi Rhodes, Stephanie Miller, and the late Ed Schultz. But a conservative purchased those stations and got rid of Rhodes, Miller and Schultz and put Rush Limbaugh on that station.

Now there is no liberal or progressive voice on free radio. Our free radio is controlled by conservatives.

SOLUTION

Reinstate the Fairness Doctrine with changes to take into account today's social media on the internet. Let me clear something up that many people don't understand. The Constitution only concerns protecting people from government and not corporations or individuals. If Facebook and Twitter kick Trump off of his account for inciting a riot, that is their choice and it is NOT a violation of his constitutional rights as many of the morons claim.

At the same time, they want to be able to say anything they want on a website, they want to hold the company owning the site to be liable for what anyone says on it. They can't have it both ways. You can't allow someone to tell lies on a website and then hold the company liable yet not allow the company to regulate what is said on its sites.

The reinstituted Fairness Doctrine must include radio, television, print media, and the internet. It is a different world now and the internet plays the largest role in how people receive information.

FINANCIAL REFORM

This country will not move forward until there is real corporate reform. If the economic meltdown hasn't shown Americans that corporations cannot be left to decide what is best, then I don't know what will. During the reign of President George W. Bush, Wall Streeters and banksters pretty much did whatever they wanted to do.

Investors should have the assurance that the money they invest in a publicly traded corporation will be used wisely. Instead of using investor funds to grow the company, CEOs took the money and blew it on corporate jets, million -dollar artwork for their offices, and lavish parties. Since they can't be trusted, we have to place limits on their extravagances.

American Airlines filed for Chapter 11 bankruptcy protection. CEO Gerard Arpey was paid almost $6 million. In 2003, the company paid secret bonuses to management a day after it announced squeezing more than $1 billion in concessions from its unions. American Airlines CEOs received bonuses at the same time the company was losing money. You can get bonuses for incompetency? Apparently so. As if that wasn't bad enough, the Trump administration gave billions of dollars to the airlines over COVID 19 when they were the primary spreaders of the disease because they refused to implement safety measures for flying to prevent the spread of the disease.

AT&T's CEO Randall Stephenson, cost the company $3 billion in his failed attempt to buy T-Mobile from Deutsche Telekom AG. If this person worked for a private company, he would probably be fired immediately. But at AT&T, he continues to draw his exorbitant salary because they need to attract "quality" people. Now Republicans will blame the government for preventing AT&T to regain its monopoly status in the telecommunications business. I had dealings with AT&T and still do because they are the only carrier in my area. They charged me for an 800 number for my business, which I never ordered. When I threatened to sue them, I was told by their employee, "Go ahead. We'll win. We're bigger than you!" I swear, that is what she said! So, I will not shed any tears over AT&T losing $3 billion dollars except for the fact that they will charge us, their customers, for their incompetence.

A Chevron executive made the decision not to replace a failed pipe at its Richmond, California refinery. That decision cost the company millions, if not billions of dollars because the pipe caused a fire which not only shut the refinery down but prevented the company from producing fuel. The problem here is that Wall Street investors demand huge profits so corporations are forced to forgo necessary repairs and maintenance. Exxon-Mobile's Torrance Refinery (since sold) had almost monthly meltdowns due to poor maintenance of the equipment, sending toxic waste into the neighboring area of residential homes. CEOs no longer make decisions based on what is best for the company or their customers, but what will satisfy the greedy Wall Street investors immediately, often to the peril of the corporation.

Most large well-established corporations can run without a CEO. The CEO's primary job is to constantly improve the product or service and keep up with the latest market demands. They should be looking at least a decade into the future to determine the direction of their corporation. The truth is that there are very few CEOs who plan for the future. They are merely on auto pilot. The lower paid workers are the ones who actually keep the company operating. Knowing that, there is no one person in the world worth $250 million a year for running a company that they did not create and that is run by the employees - not the CEO. If the President of the United States can run the whole country and influence the world on just $400,000 a year, what makes the CEOs think they are worth so much more? They aren't. The CEO of AIG couldn't even tell Congress how much exposure his firm had to the residential mortgage market. General Motors continued to produce gas guzzling muscle cars when gas was inching towards $5.00 a gallon. Tobacco companies should be looking for new products instead of pushing their tobacco overseas and getting two-year old babies hooked on their cigarettes! Honestly! There are two-year old children in Asian countries smoking packs of cigarettes per day!

Congress should enact the following legislation called the "Investor's Assurance Act." It doesn't need to be 2000 pages long. This simple plan will do. Whenever someone writes a 2000-page piece of legislation, you can be sure there is something in there that they don't want anyone to notice. (i.e. The Affordable Care Act aka Obamacare).

Originally, I felt this should only apply to publicly traded corporations, but since many of the publicly traded corporations are buying back their stock and taking the corporation private, we may have to include all corporations that have employees.

SOLUTION: INVESTOR ASSURANCE ACT

SECTION 1: EMPLOYEE COMPENSATION

Corporations that have employees must institute a profit-sharing plan for ALL employees. The base salary of the CEO cannot be more than the salary of the President of the United States. CEOs can make up any difference through profit-sharing that is available to ALL employees. Profits shall be divided three ways: One-third for shareholders. One-third for employees. One-third to remain in the corporation for development and maintenance.

WHY? Profit sharing by all employees will help eliminate theft by employees because they would only be stealing from themselves. It will increase productivity because if the company does better, the employee will earn more money. The corporation will produce a better product or service because employees will care about the company and know that if they produce a bad product or service, they will lose customers. By sharing profits with all employees, those employees will go out and spend the money they are earning and stimulate the economy.

This will also fix the problem of income inequality. People have to be able to earn enough money to support their families without holding down several jobs just to earn enough to pay the rent, while the CEOs buy $250 million dollar homes. In the 1950's, the father had a good job and earned a decent wage so that the mother could stay home with the children. The father got home in time to eat with the family. CEOs did not earn the outrageous salaries that they earn today.

SECTION 2: FINANCIAL STATEMENT DISCLOSURE

Financial statements of publicly traded corporations need to have a separate line for officer salaries and any and all other compensation. Furthermore, salaries over $400,000 and the accompanying additional compensation will not be tax deductible. The corporation will have to pay taxes on the income BEFORE extra CEO compensation.

WHY? Investors need to know how much of the income is being spent on CEO compensation. As an investor, I want to know why the income was so small. Did the CEO take all the profit so that investors got very little of the income?

If the corona virus pandemic has taught us anything it is that CEOs and the government are way overpaid for what they do. We were supposed to get "experienced" people for those exorbitant salaries. Yet the airline industry cried like babies because they suddenly lost money due to a pandemic that they mainly caused by not instituting any safeguards for the spread of the virus on their airplanes. But because our politicians are in their pockets, they received billions of dollars for their incompetency.

SECTION 3 STOCK OPTIONS

Stock options by employees should be absolutely eliminated in publicly traded corporations.

WHY? This is insider trading. If the CEOs don't have inside information about the financial status of the company, then they have no business running it. If they DO know this information, then they have no business being able to control thousands of shares of the company stock because they will know information that you and other investors don't have access to.

SECTION 4 COMMODITY TRADING

Commodity trading is betting on the future of the product of a corporation. It should be banned period.

WHY? Allowing someone to bet on gasoline or food creates shortages and permits the manipulation of prices. OPEC for example, stopped producing oil after the demand for oil dropped. By holding back production, they will have less oil on the market and then the price of that oil will increase. Can't you see where this is going? Do you really want a Wall Street investor determining how much you pay for oil or food? Yet that is exactly what is happening. It was just recently announced that they were allowing investors to treat WATER as a commodity and allow trading in water.

If someone wants to invest in cotton, then let them buy stock in a company that manufacturers cotton. The same applies to oil or any other commodity that deals in necessities.

We have to stop this constant betting. What's next? Betting on how long your elderly neighbor will live and then killing him because your bet says he dies today? Could happen.

SECTION 5 MONOPOLIES

A monopoly occurs when a company attempts to destroy competition. Years ago, the government broke up AT&T because they owned most of the telephone companies. But over the years, they are almost back where they were.

Forget about reading books and newspapers. Just read the comic "Dilbert" for all you need to know about business. A recent cartoon had Dilbert's boss justifying being a monopoly by saying, "No. We are not a monopoly because other companies could compete with us if they wanted." When asked what would happen if they tried, he said "As soon as they got some traction, we'd buy them and shut them down." Then the employee says, "So they would fail every time?" The boss says, "But they could try."

It is especially troubling when they are buying up media companies and use that platform to skew the news in the favor of their candidates. I can't find a single radio station anymore that isn't conservative. There used to be Randi Rhodes and Stephanie Miller where you could call in with a non-conservative view and be heard. Try calling Glenn Beck with an opinion other than his and see if you get on the air. In fact, they don't even want to hear from you anymore.

There needs to be a strict limit on just how many companies in a market one company can own. But even better, we need an attorney with some real guts to file a legal action preventing corporations from buying another corporation. Why? Because, as the Supreme Court ruled, corporations are "people" and people cannot buy and sell other people. Here is how you do it. You find a small business owner who has one or two employees. If they are relatives, then they are not treated the same as other employees. You have the owner file an action to buy the employees so he can own them and avoid the employee status. If the court objects to the purchase of human people, then site Citizens United as the basis for allowing the purchase! See what they think about that!

SECTION 6 CONGRESSIONAL EXEMPTION FROM INSIDER TRADING

Why we even need to pass this legislation speaks for itself as to the integrity of those we have elected to Congress. Congress conveniently exempted its members from insider trading laws. If your congressperson has information on an investment that you and I do not have access to, they are exempt from that information being considered insider trading. If a certain piece of legislation they are proposing is going to impact a certain industry, they can buy or sell stock in those industries before the legislation takes effect and before you and I know about the legislation.

This exemption needs to go as well as every congressional member who voted for it! Representative Nancy Pelosi, when asked by Steve Croft of CBS "60 Minutes" about insider trading by Congress, she simply replied, "What's your point?" Shame on her and all the others in Congress just like her.

IN SUMMARY

At the present time (before corporations take themselves out of the stock market), if a corporation is private, they can pay themselves whatever they want because there will be no risk to investors. There has to be a price to pay for taking money from the public and there has to be accountability. We need to stop rewarding incompetence.

WHO WILL OPPOSE IT

Those who benefit from greed will oppose this legislation. As Lee Iacocca once said (referring to how much money people need), "You never get enough."

GUN CONTROL

During the time of the Second Amendment, there were not the state and city police departments that exist today to protect us. The Second Amendment states that a well- regulated Militia was necessary to the security of a free state. It gave the people the right to keep and bear arms.

While it is argued that since we have state and local security forces, it is no longer necessary to grant individuals the right to bear arms.

I am not so sure I agree with that philosophy. Let me say that I am a gun owner and keep it for my own protection. If someone is breaking into my home, by the time I call the police and they arrive, I would probably be dead if I didn't have a gun.

The question is how powerful should the arms be that we are allowed to possess. Do we need assault weapons? I guess that would depend upon where you live. If you live in an area where there are gangs that use assault weapons, then you could argue that you should have the right to own an assault weapon.

So, the issue of whether or not we are permitted to own and possess arms is pretty much indisputable.

The NRA has done a poor job of presenting their case. The

problem with all the shootings isn't the gun. It's the person that owns the gun. I have owned my gun for over 20 years and that gun has never killed anyone. Nor have I.

The problem is keeping weapons out of the hands of the crazies. I want to clear something up. There are people who are mentally ill who pose no threat to anyone. I am not referring to them. When I say crazies, I mean those who fall in with violent groups or are drug addicts. They often have no history of an actual mental illness.

Since the ACLU opposes confining people with mental issues, you have no way of stopping crazies from getting weapons. Until you allow a mental health expert to certify that a person should not have access to weapons you won't prevent them from obtaining weapons. I have no problem with preventing felons and people with mental issues from owning weapons.

Let me explain why the NRA opposes gun registration. In some countries, when the government knew a person had a gun, they would take it from them to prevent any insurrection. I am not sure that a few people with weapons would stop a government takeover by an enemy.

The problem is keeping those arms out of the hands of crazies and convicted felons.

SOLUTION

In order to purchase a firearm, there needs to be a background check on the person. Do they have a criminal record? Do they have a history of mental disorders? If so, then they cannot purchase a firearm.

The criminal part of the check is easy. But defining what mental disorder qualifies them to be denied a weapon is tricky. Also, it is not a sure way of preventing people with mental issues from getting weapons because a lot of the mass shooters had no history of mental disorders. They may have been crazy but never sought help for it and relatives never turned them in for their craziness. Making violent threats should certainly qualify as a qualification for denial of a firearm.

HEALTHCARE

Once again, I presented my plan for healthcare to my Senators and to President Obama and was ignored. So, we ended up with Obamacare, a plan with serious defects. The worst part is the requirement that people purchase health insurance without putting any limitations on the amount insurance companies can charge for those plans. Republicans recently removed that requirement, but they did not make any attempt to regulate what insurance companies can charge either.

The Republicans considered the part requiring people to purchase health insurance *socialism* saying you can't force people to purchase something. Oh, if only they had studied history in school. President George Washington, in the Militia Act of 1792, required all males between the ages of 18 and 45 to purchase a musket, bayonet and belt, two spare flints, a knapsack, shot-pouch and powder horn, twenty balls suited to the bore of his rifle, and a quarter of a pound of powder. The Supreme Court might refresh their history lessons as well.

SOLUTIONS:

1. HEALTHCARE TAX

So here is my plan. We institute a national healthcare tax on those corporations whose products cause catastrophic illnesses. We know who they are because we require them to place warnings on their products. We know what the costs are for catastrophic illnesses. Those costs are divided among all the corporations causing the illnesses and are paid through a healthcare tax on the corporations. For accidents and other injuries determined to be caused by alcohol, the alcohol industry will be RESPONSIBLE for those costs.

The Healthcare Tax Fund is to be exclusively used to reimburse insurance companies or self-insured individuals for those catastrophic illnesses and alcohol related injuries. Any monies not paid out are refunded to the corporations contributing to the Fund.

The alcohol industry will be responsible for many injuries and illnesses. There are many deaths and catastrophic injuries caused by drunk drivers and drunks who beat up on someone. It is simply wrong to make the insurance companies pay for those claims and it is wrong to make others pay into the fund for claims that are specific to the alcohol industry. The tax for the alcohol industry includes drunk driving costs and other alcohol related injuries or illnesses. These costs are for medical expenses only. The individual causing these injuries would still be liable for their actions in a court of law.

If Republicans want human people to be RESPONSIBLE for their own healthcare, then corporate people must be held RESPONSIBLE for the healthcare costs their products cause. Fair. Right?

2. REVISE PRESCRIPTION DRUG BENEFIT LEGISLATION

As a gift to the pharmaceutical industry, Congress prohibited Medicare from being able to negotiate prices for prescriptions. This ended up costing us much more than it should and the greedy pharmaceutical companies raised prices as much as 6000%. Marathon Pharmaceuticals sells deflazacort, a drug to treat children with muscular dystrophy, for $1000 - $2000 in Europe and Canada, but charges $89,000 in the U.S. Yet Congress has done nothing to fix price gouging!

We need to amend this legislation to permit Medicare to negotiate the same way the military can negotiate for their prescriptions.

3. NATIONAL ID CARD FOR BENEFITS

Medicare fraud is a big problem and could be solved with a National ID Card that has a photo and a thumbprint on it so that it cannot be used by anyone other than the person to whom it was issued.

4. BAN DOCTORS CONVICTED OF FRAUD

Doctors who are convicted of Medicare Fraud should be banned for life from participating in Medicare.

BENEFITS OF THE PLAN

1. The beauty of the plan is that the costs to the government are minimal. Their only cost is to manage the Fund.

2. This frees up insurance companies to provide affordable health care to cover minor illnesses or injuries thus preventing hospitals from having to eat non-insured patient costs.

3. In addition, all products coming into the U.S. would be subject to this tax, if said products are known to cause cancer

or other catastrophic illnesses or injuries. China alone would bring in billions of dollars!

4. Since corporations are RESPONSIBLE for the healthcare costs their products cause, they will also care about rising healthcare costs and so the industry will be self-regulating. If doctors are charging exorbitant fees, the corporations can pressure them to reduce costs. The government stays out of the process.

5. If corporations have to pay for the healthcare costs related to their products, they just might either stop producing their toxic products or find a safer way to manufacture them, which will clean up the environment!

WHO WILL OPPOSE IT

Obviously, the oil companies, the tobacco, industry, the alcohol industry, the chemical industry, the pharmaceutical industry and the politicians who are in the pockets of those industries.

The providers who have been scamming the system won't like this plan.

Finally, there will be those who are afraid of "big government" knowing everything about you through the National ID Card. I've got news for you – the corporations you deal with know more about you than the government ever will. Your resistance to a National ID Card, which could also be used for voting, is lame, at best.

HOMELESSNESS

I am going to use Los Angeles as an example as I have lived here for 40 years and am more familiar with it than any other city. Last year the city spent $619 million on homelessness and we only have 58,000 homeless people. Do the math. That is $10+ million per homeless person and they are still on the street! They could have given every single homeless person $200,000 with the restriction that they cannot return to the street and saved us a lot of money. The drug addicts and alcoholics would have blown it and probably OD's solving that problem. The people needing a home would have been able to rent one. People needing jobs would have had a respite before the economy comes back and those with mental and health problems could afford to seek help.

Instead, we are $619 million poorer and the homeless are still on the street. I have to ask Mayor Garcetti – where the hell did the money go? Oh, sorry mayor, I forgot about your planning department and Councilman Alex Huizar allegedly taking bribes from developers.

I have been in Los Angeles long enough to remember when there were dozens of old apartment buildings near downtown and the low-income people who worked downtown could afford to live near their jobs. But then the city bulldozed all those apartments so that they could beautify downtown with the likes of Staples Center and all the luxury high- rise apartments. This meant money in the hands of our politicians from the bribes. Then they had the audacity to complain about all the homeless people showing up on the streets and they actually were surprised. Where the hell did you think the people who lived in the apartments would go?

That was bad enough but then the ACLU got involved in the prison population and Trump let certain prisoners out of prison. Guess where they ended up? Now I could have told them for free where the "new" homeless people came from, but they probably paid someone else to do a study. Do we not have anyone with COMMON SENSE?

There are several reasons for homelessness. Some are the person's own fault and others are not.

1. Loss of Job
2. Cannot afford to pay rent
3. Illness
4. Mental Illness
5. Drug Addiction/Alcoholism
6. Veteran

SOLUTIONS

1. LOSS OF JOB – Put these people to work for pay doing government jobs like, oh I don't know, how about fixing the pot holes in our roads? Hire them to clean our streets or other jobs that our government employees just can't seem to get to.

2. CANNOT PAY RENT – Bring back the affordable housing to downtown. Better yet, when you can't rent out the extravagant high-rise apartments, reduce the rent and let the people who used to live downtown move into them.

3. ILLNESS – People who are physically sick or disabled should not be out on the streets. Turn vacant buildings into housing for them and provide them with medical care so they can

recover. I can't even imagine what it must be like to be on the street in a wheel chair and sick with no help in sight. I have to ask this question of all the Christians who claim to care so much for people – where are you?

4. MENTAL ILLNESS – While it is true that you can help some mentally ill people with medications, unless you are with them 24/7 you can't be sure they will take their meds. Even people who have a mentally ill person in their homes cannot be sure they are taking their meds. When they don't take them is when they end up in trouble. The only sure way that someone takes their meds is in a locked facility. It was the ACLU's opposition to this that led to Ronald Reagan releasing the mentally ill from locked facilities. I think it is more humane to put someone who is a danger to themselves or others in a locked facility rather than on the street where they can be raped or otherwise abused.

5. DRUG ADDICTION/ALCOHOLISM – This is a tough one because most of these people don't want to change their behavior. That is the nature of addiction. Celebrities have spent millions of dollars on recovery programs to no avail. A few months later they are either back in rehab or dead. Betty Ford Center seems to have the best success rate at 80% so perhaps they should all have to go through that program. Addicts want to be on the streets because that is how they get the money for their addiction. Allowing them that freedom allows their addiction. Did I mention that the rehab will be paid by the alcohol and drug companies who enable the addict?

6. VETERANS – This will be an easy one. The corporations who benefited from the veterans' service to their country have to pay for whatever it is that the veteran needs to return to normal or as near to normal as possible given what they have gone through in war. This should be through the Veterans Administration.

WHO WILL OPPOSE IT

Obviously, the alcohol and drug corporations will oppose it because it will cost them money for the havoc their products cause people. In addition, rehab scammers will oppose it because they make a lot of money by keeping people in their rehab programs that don't work. Don't forget the ACLU also because people have the right to be homeless!

IMMIGRATION

There is nothing wrong with hiring immigrants if the workers have legal worker status and if the company pays them minimum wage or better. It is the companies and farmers who hire workers that they know are illegal that are the problem. They exploit them by paying them less than minimum wage and fail to provide safe equipment, working conditions, and housing.

All the chatter about building this mega fence on our southern border is nonsense. This didn't work for China and it won't work for us. Already, the border patrol has found tunnels under the areas that have a fence. The illegals also enter the country via boats. Someone used the excuse that we put fences in our yards to keep people out. Well, no we put fences for privacy. We know full well that if a criminal wants to get into our yard, they just have to hop the fence. Why my fence didn't even keep my Border Collie from escaping when I first got her. She dug a hole under it!

When President Trump promised his supporters a magnificent wall and Mexico would pay for it, I suggested he pay for it himself and get reimbursed from Mexico.

The claim that illegal immigrants are taking jobs from U.S. citizens is not entirely true. Most of those jobs, our people simply will not do. When was the last time you saw a white person in the fields bent over picking strawberries? These people are just trying to provide a decent life for their families. Most of them are not criminals except for their illegal status. Yes, there are also drug dealers crossing the borders, but that is a whole other problem.

This is all about supply and demand. When the jobs dried up in the U.S. illegal immigration declined. When the Republicans speak of keeping our borders safe, they are speaking about Mexicans and others from Latin America. They say and do nothing about terrorists entering the company via air or entering through Canada. So, yes, this is a racial thing. None of the 9/11 terrorists came across the border from Mexico.

Immigrants come to the U.S. for two reasons. They come for jobs and some of them come to deal drugs.

SOLUTION – JOB SEEKERS

This is very simple. Companies that need to hire people from another country must go through the proper channels to obtain approval from the government to bring in such workers. But the problem is that companies don't want to go through the proper channels because they would have to pay workers minimum wages and provide safe working conditions.

The only way to stop this practice is to fine the employers so heavily that it will no longer be profitable for them to hire illegal workers. Yes, you will probably pay more for fruit but you have to choose your poison. Do you want to deal with illegal immigrants or do you want to pay more for your fruit?

The very rich also employ known illegal workers in their homes and yards because they don't want to pay into Social Security and other taxes required if they hire a legal worker. They often threaten the illegal workers with deportation if they complain about long hours or unsafe conditions. We need to provide a safe place where these workers can go to report these so-called employers without fear of deportation. Then we need to fine the employers.

SOLUTION – DRUG DEALERS

Once again, if our citizens weren't addicted to illegal drugs, the drug dealers from across the border wouldn't be trying to get their drugs into our country. Again, it is simply supply and demand.

I have a feeling that our government doesn't care about illegal drugs because the illegal drug industry helps keep our economy going. Although drug dealers don't pay taxes, they do buy a lot of stuff with their profits. If they are making money that way, the government doesn't have to pay for their welfare or try to find jobs for them. The government looks the other way and occasionally will conduct a drug bust just to let us think they are on top of the problem. But they are not. Otherwise we wouldn't have so many people addicted to drugs.

We should be concerned because many of the people addicted to drugs have long-lasting effects that result in bizarre behavior. They kill people because they imagine something or someone in their head tells them to kill someone. This is probably the hardest problem we have to solve because the person doesn't want to stop using drugs and because there aren't any drug treatment programs that will guarantee that they will cure drug addiction. There are only opportunists who will claim rehab but just take the person's money. This is the one problem for which I can't offer a solution. Well, at least not one that would be accepted. Well, I do have one suggestion – make the drug supplier RESPONSIBLE and charge them with murder when they supply the drugs that a person overdoses on because *but for* the supplier, the person wouldn't be doing drugs. Sue them in civil court. When you remove the profit from a bad behavior, you remove the incentive.

JUDICIAL REFORM

There is no question that black people are treated differently than white people by law enforcement. All you have to do is look at the way white domestic terrorists were allowed into the U.S. Capitol and allowed to destroy it and cause the death of a police officer. Then look at the way the Black Lives Matter people were met at the Lincoln Memorial with armed guards surrounding the building.

I wonder, as do many people, why cops can take a white mass shooter into custody when they know he has an arsenal of high-powered weapons yet will shoot and kill a black kid who is running away from them. I would be more afraid and more apt to shoot the mass murderer than I would someone running away, but then that's just me.

The shooting of Breonna Taylor was tragic. While the cops acted after her boyfriend shot at them, that was not the real problem with this murder. The cops failed to do due diligence and verify that the person they were seeking with their warrant still lived there! He didn't and the cops should have known that before they obtained that warrant. This is the liability in this case. Because someone didn't do their job, a young woman is dead unnecessarily.

I like to think that most cops are good cops and really want to do a good job. But there are also many bad cops out there who are just pure evil. The riots at the Democratic Convention in Chicago were determined to have been started by the Chicago police. The cops and the FBI murdered Fred Hampton, a black man who was a leader in the Black Panthers. It is necessary to weed out those types of cops and put them in prison where they belong and don't give them protected status. Let them deal with the other prisoners the way we have to deal with them.

After what Trump has done in pardoning everyone including his family for any crimes they may have committed, this needs to be addressed. Also, to consider is the question of "Does a president have the right to pardon himself?"

Most presidents have pardoned questionable felons and that is just wrong. Why? Because we go to great time and expense to try someone of a crime and a jury decides guilt or innocence. Why then should a president or governor come along and say, "The hell with that. You are free to go and your record is wiped clean." It is no wonder people don't want to waste their time serving on a jury.

Another issue that needs to be clarified is the definition of treason. No one ever seems to decide just what constitutes treason and that is because our founders left that area very vague. Surely attacking our Capitol and attempting to murder representatives and senators is treason and organizing such an attack should also be treason.

SOLUTIONS

POLICE

    A. Body Cameras – Every police officer and every police car must have body cameras that are operating. Failure to turn on the cameras during a police activity will result in the failure of the officer to be able to claim self-defense or a threat to their life. This is for the benefit of the officers as well as the suspect because much of the action occurs before individuals turn on their cameras so we are only getting one side of the confrontation.

B. Officers must all go through firearms classes and be rated at a certain level to be able to carry a gun. Any officer that has to shoot a suspect seven or more times clearly should not have a gun. It should not be "become a cop, get a gun." They should have to earn that gun and know how to use it!

C. New training and sensitivity training so that officers who display prejudices are given special training so that their performance does not utilize their prejudices.

D. Officers cited for proven offenses must have their records publicly revealed and after a certain number of offenses, they must be removed from the force.

E. There should be a separate part of the police department that only handles people with mental issues or drug issues that are non-violent. This will allow the regular police officers to handle serious crimes and allow someone knowledgeable about mental health to handle those calls. But there will be times when a complaint is made and the officers do not know ahead of time that the person has a mental or drug problem. But if the dispatcher can ascertain right away if there is a drug or mental problem involved, they could determine who to send to the scene.

PROSECUTION

A. Prosecutors and defense attorneys must also undergo sensitivity training to mitigate their prejudices.

B. Laws need to be changed to prevent someone getting a life sentence for a third strike theft when they were stealing food because they were hungry.

C. Laws need to be applied evenly without regard to wealth or standing in the community. There has to be set sentences for a crime regardless of who commits it. The idea that people get away with rape because they are wealthy or a member of the clergy is disgusting.

D. We need to remove all statutes of limitations. Simply waiting out a crime doesn't make it right nor does it grant the victim any justice. If you commit the crime, you should have to live with the fear of getting caught the rest of your life. The child is not "spared" suffering because the Catholic Church did not report the rape by a priest to the local criminal authorities as required by law.

E. Pardons should be abolished by the president or anyone else. If someone is indeed innocent then let them be proven so in a court of law. The fact that the president can pardon people who committed crimes is unthinkable.

F. Ban concurrent sentencing. This is nothing more than a two for one sale on criminal activity. It means if you rob a store, steal a car, and injure someone, you get to serve the sentence for robbery, auto theft, and bodily injury all at the same time instead of each one individually.

G. Prisoners sentenced to mental facilities instead of prison, if ever deemed "sane" must then serve the normal sentence for their original crime.

TREASON

Simply establish a definition of what is actually treason. While there is a fine line between treason and the right to protest, there are certain actions that are not part of a protest. Murdering of government officials should not be part of a protest. Trump also encouraged his traitors to kidnap the governor of Michigan. Don't forget that and that they would probably have killed her had their plan been executed.

NOTE TO SUSPECTED CRIMINALS and PROTESTORS

All I can say is don't run from the police! You know how this is going to turn out and it isn't going to go well for you. When you run from them you get their adrenalin going and the more you run the faster their adrenalin goes. When you finally stop, they are not only going to be angry but not thinking rationally.

In defense of police, they face the worst of society every single day, all day long. You may be upset because they are stopping you but don't pour gas on the fire by running or fighting with them. You probably won't win.

If you are protesting then don't become violent and start looting and burning down buildings and breaking windows. That action doesn't help your cause at all. In fact, it just reinforces the belief that you are a bunch of thugs and your message will get lost in your actions and you will accomplish nothing.

It needs to be said here that the government is not beyond planting rioters among protesters. Just read about how the FBI murdered Fred Hampton during the 70's protests. It has also been reported that riot gear was dropped off at areas where the Black Lives Matter people were going to protest and that later cars would pull up with people who started burning stores, breaking windows and stealing merchandise. This was NOT the Black Lives Matter people, but was done by someone to discredit them and make people think that they were ALL looters.

★ ★ ★ ★ ★

MILITARY

PROBLEM 1 PURPOSE OF THE MILITARY

The military is supposed to be for the protection of our country from attack by another country. However, it was hijacked by corporations to provide protection for corporate overseas operations. We don't need 50,000 military personnel in Germany. I am pretty sure we defeated Hitler some time ago and Germany is a democratic country. Our primary purpose for troops in Germany is to protect corporate interests in Germany and other European countries.

On February 14, 1945, Franklin D. Roosevelt initiated an oil-for-security relationship with Saudi Arabia. In 1959 the CIA hired Saddam Hussein to shoot Iraqi Prime Minister Qasim, but Hussein failed.

In 1980 President Carter had Hussein invade Iran and started the Iran-Iraq War because Iranian leader, Khomeini threatened Saudi Arabian oil.

Under Presidents Reagan and Bush Sr., the Center for Disease Control supplied Saddam Hussein with viruses, bacteria, etc. including West Nile Virus. Later the U.S. would provide arms to Osama Bin Laden in the Afghanistan War with Russia. Bin Laden, knowing that the U.S. would eventually abandon them, stock piled the weapons we gave him and these weapons were used against our troops in Afghanistan.

If you still have any doubt that your sons and daughters were killed or mutilated in the Iraq-Afghanistan wars because of oil, you need look no further than to learn that in 2011 Exxon Mobil signed a deal with the Iraqi Kurds to develop the oil fields in West Qurna.

President George W. Bush said Osama Bin Laden hated us because of our freedom. Nothing could be further from the truth. Bin Laden issued a statement that he hated us because we occupied sacred land with our military. After Operation Desert Shield in 1990, the U.S. left troops in Saudi Arabia to protect Saudi oil shipping lanes. In 2003, President George W. Bush removed most troops from Saudi Arabia because many Muslims were upset at our bases being located on holy sites….after 9/11!

It shouldn't surprise anyone that we take what we want. After all, our country was founded by settlers who took the country from the Indians. Then when we wanted some of Mexico's land, we took it also. We have allowed corporations to turn us into the bully who goes into a country and takes whatever it is that the corporations want.

SOLUTION TO PROBLEM 1

Since Republicans are big on everyone accepting RESPONSIBILITY for themselves and since the Supreme Court and Mitt Romney believe that corporations are *people* then corporations need to accept RESPONSIBILITY for their own security in other countries. This will free up trillions of dollars in costs related to the military. The U.S. will only pay for the military that is necessary to protect our homeland and not corporate interests in other countries. Many of these corporations pay no taxes either and those that do, pay even less thanks to President Trump and his spineless Republican shills in Congress.

You and I pay for corporate security – with our money and the lives of our young people. This is the Republican and corporate plan that PRIVATIZES THE PROFITS AND SOCIALIZES THE LOSSES!

PROBLEM 2 MILITARY SPENDING

One of the greatest presidents and generals was Dwight D. Eisenhower. He urged Congress to end the Cold War with the Soviets by saying, "Every gun that is made, every warship launched, every rocket fired signifies a theft from those who hunger and are not fed, those who are cold and are not clothed. This world…is spending the sweat of its laborers, the genius of its scientists, the hopes of its children. The cost of one modern heavy bomber is…a modern brick school in more than 30 cities. It is two electric power plants, each serving a town of 60,000 population. It is two fine, fully equipped hospitals. It is some 50 miles of concrete pavement. We pay for a single fighter plane with a half-million bushels of wheat. We pay for a single destroyer with new homes that could have housed more than 8,000 people…This is not a way of life at all…Under the cloud of threatening war, it is humanity hanging from a cross of iron."

Congress funds the military without questioning anything and often with no-bid contracts with suppliers. This has to stop. Two women figured out that if they billed the military for under one million dollars, they would be paid without question and made millions of dollars until they were finally caught.

It is unconscionable that no one has been prosecuted for war profiteering during the Iraq-Afghanistan Wars. Cher - yes, the entertainer – personally purchased safety inserts for the soldiers' helmets to prevent brain injuries. Our soldiers were sent to those wars with equipment that the military knew was inferior. They were given inferior food and water. Halliburton, Dick Cheney's former employer, was RESPONSIBLE for much of the war profiteering and continues in that position today. Only they are no longer headquartered in the U.S.

Congress has acted as if they were playing with Monopoly money. They just kept signing off on expenditures without questioning where the money was going. There were pallets of $1,000 bills sent to Iraq – for what? For a long period of time no one had any idea where these pallets were located.

When it comes to cutting military costs, the Republicans want to cut the costs to veterans' benefits. They don't want to have to pay for the soldier who returned with no legs or arms and will never be able to work again. They treat the injured soldiers like a piece of garbage because they are no longer of any use to them. President Trump, who used veterans as pawns in his election bid, didn't even attend a single ceremony on Veteran's Day 2018 because it was *raining*. What if our soldiers had said, "I can't fight today, it's raining"? Even worse, Trump referred to the soldiers as "losers and suckers."

SOLUTION TO PROBLEM 2

There needs to be a private entity to review all military spending and to test products that are purchased to ascertain that they do what they are supposed to do. There should never be another $5,000 hammer!

Any corporation found to have fraudulently supplied items to the military should be banned from ever bidding on another contract. The persons RESPONSIBLE should also be banned because it is all too easy for them to just form a new corporation tomorrow and start bidding all over again. We need to take names and hold those guilty of war-profiteering or fraud accountable and punish them severely.

There should NEVER be a no-bid contract.

There needs to be an accurate system put in place for verification that items purchased are received and accounted for at all times.

PROBLEM 3 THE DRAFT

President Franklin Roosevelt signed the Selective Training and Service Act of 1940 which created the military draft and established the Selective Service System as an independent Federal agency. From 1948 until 1973, men were drafted to fill vacancies in the armed forces which were not filled voluntarily.

In 1973, the draft was ended and the U.S. became an all-volunteer military. The Bush administration refused to reinstitute the draft during the Iraq-Afghanistan wars. Why? Because of the changes to the draft, the wealthy could no longer claim a student deferment indefinitely. They would have had to serve along with everyone else. Instead of handling the draft equitably, they left it a volunteer military but made the volunteers serve over and over again. As a result, the volunteers were stressed to the max with the multiple deployments.

The Bush Administration also knew that the people would really oppose the war if they were forced to enlist. By maintaining the volunteer aspect, they just burned out the existing volunteers when more did not step up to go to war. This is the real atrocity of the oil wars. Thousands of men and women were either killed or horribly mutilated by the roadside bombs in Iraq and Afghanistan because they were put in vehicles that were not safe. When I see pictures of these brave soldiers without limbs or parts of their faces, it just breaks my heart and then I get furious with my country and the spineless members of Congress for causing this mayhem – just for the sake of oil!

I can't leave the subject of the draft without mentioning something that has irritated me for years and that is the treatment of Vietnam Veterans and Jane Fonda. First of all, the soldiers serving in the Vietnam War were drafted. It was not a voluntary army and they did what they were forced to do by their commanders. That is simply the way the system works. Each soldier does not have the right to do what they think is right. They have to follow orders. As a result of that policy, they did horrible things in Vietnam by killing innocent women and children at the Mai Lai Massacre. Jane Fonda went there to use her celebrity status to shed light into the problem. But what Republicans always love to do, **they shot the messenger to distract from the message.** Jane Fonda remains one of the very few people I respect in this world because she put her job and life on the line to do the right thing. It was right to expose what our government was doing.

As far as the way the Vietnam Veterans were treated when they returned, that was totally wrong. First of all, they didn't have a choice whether to go to Vietnam or not; well unless you consider fleeing to Canada a choice. Rightfully so, some of their commanders were

     SHIRLEY CONLEY

prosecuted for what they made these soldiers do in Vietnam. But the returning soldiers didn't deserve the treatment they received and suffered mentally for it. They deserve a formal apology. And so does Jane Fonda!

SOLUTION TO PROBLEM 3

Reinstitute the draft with NO exceptions. I think if everyone has to experience war then, perhaps they will hesitate to get their country involved in one. Also, it is just wrong to keep a segment of society uneducated and poor just so they will be available to fight corporate wars. Perhaps if we had sent Liz Cheney to the front lines her father would have been less loose with the soldiers' lives. Or perhaps not. The man has no heart.

RACISM

First, we stole the country from the Indians. However, we have compensated them for it in a number of ways and continue to compensate them. Then we went to war with Japan and rounded up all the Japanese-Americans and sent them to internment camps, taking their money and property in the process. Ronald Reagan gave payments to the Japanese-Americans who were interned for a total of $1.6 billion dollars.

British profiteers in 1619 brought the first black people to our country and sold them off as slaves. This practice continued – kidnapping black people from Africa and selling them in the U.S. as slaves – until the end of the Civil War in 1861.

The Civil War was the bloodiest war in history with 625,000 people killed from 1861 to 1865. The Southern states wanted to keep slaves and the Northern ones did not. But the South lost the war so in reality, the Rebel flag is a symbol of losers! But white southerners still cling to the flag as if they had won. And sadly, still cling to the belief that white people are superior to black people or any other people of color.

Now, the flag has nothing to do with the Civil War. These white racists are not carrying the flag because they want to own slaves again.

They have turned it into a symbol of hatred for black people. It is for this reason that the rebel flag is seen by most Americans as a symbol of hatred and not about a Civil War loss.

White racists have displayed the rebel flag as they hanged black people, dragged them through the streets, burned their homes and churches, denied them access to businesses and education, and refused service to them. This is not what American should be about and it is for this reason that the rebel flag should not be displayed. It's time to put it back into history where it belongs.

It is bad enough that this country kidnapped human beings and sold them as slaves. But while they may have certain freedoms, they are truly not free yet. Racists continue to treat black people differently and not in a good way. The black people continue to struggle today for some semblance of equality and that should not be necessary.

I had hoped that over the years people would grow up and realize that we are all people and deserve equality. But this racial hatred is embedded in these people and they are passing it down from generation to generation. How they can claim to be religious and not treat all of God's children equally is puzzling. I guess they read a different Bible than I did but my guess is that they don't read it at all.

Trump has brought racism back to life just as some people were beginning to understand that no one race is actually superior. But he loves the racists. Trump is a good example of a white person that is NOT superior. He will go down in history as the worst president ever! At least Nixon had the decency to resign but then Nixon admitted that he had committed a crime. Trump will not.

General William Sherman was said to have ordered that slaves be given 40 acres of land and a mule. But after President Lincoln was assassinated, and President Andrew Johnson took over, Johnson reversed the order. Nothing was ever done.

We have given compensation to all other races but not the black people and we have done the most horrible things to them. Even worse, we continue to do horrible things to them.

In an odd way, the white racists have unwittingly done a favor for some black people. By calling them "inferior" and making them think they aren't as good as white people, they have given black people an incentive to do better and they have risen to the occasion. When President Obama was elected, I wrote a poem called "When Given the Chance" about how black people surpassed white people almost every time they were *given the chance.*

In fact, when given the chance, black people kicked your white asses! When given the chance in music they gave us Whitney Houston, Duke Ellington, and Denyce Graves. When given the chance in sports, they gave us Kobe Bryant, Mohammad Ali, Hank Aaron, and Jim Brown. When given the chance in politics, they gave us Barbara Jordan and Barack Obama. When given the chance in entertainment, they gave us Oprah Winfrey and Tyler Perry. What have YOU done that makes YOU superior?

Part of correcting the problems black people face will be solved if we institute my ideas for schools so that all people will receive the same education. That will make a huge difference in the minority communities. When the schools are bad and children can't learn, they turn to crime and drugs which are the only other things available in their communities. Don't complain about crime in those areas if you don't want to fix the problems. White people complain about crime in the black areas, yet they don't give them the same opportunities to better their plight. In fact, for many years, they denied education to black people.

It seems like our country always has to have some race or country to demonize. For a while it shifted from black people to brown people, mainly Mexicans. But now it is back to black people but since the pandemic, they have added Asian people.

I had hoped that over two hundred years the younger generations would drop the hatred but they haven't. It didn't stop with one generation. They just taught the next generation to hate. Biographer Jean Guerrero stated this very well when she said, "I grew up with this anti-immigration hostility too – then I GREW OUT OF IT!" Unfortunately, many of you haven't grown out of it and just pass the hatred down from generation to generation. Just like the Hatfields and the McCoys, who after generations of hatred for each other, didn't really know why they originally hated each other.

I grew up on a farm fifty miles east of Cleveland and we had no black people in the town and they were always referred to by the n-word. It wasn't necessarily derogatory. It was just what they were called. Once I moved out of Ohio, I realized that it wasn't a name that I should use and unless they really pissed me off, I did not refer to them by the n-word. But when this black guy slashed the convertible top of my sports car, I called him every name I could think of including a reference to his relationship with his mother.

SOLUTION TO RACISM

First, we have to fix the education system as I mentioned in the education section. ALL children have to have access to the same QUALITY of education. Perhaps what we should do is mandate that students from Beverly Hills High attend a school in Compton and students from Compton attend a school in Beverly Hills. Then let's evaluate their learning and see who is better educated! You would have to mandate this because no one in their right mind would choose to go to school in Compton over Beverly Hills.

I happen to live in a very diverse area. There is not a dominance of one race over the other and you know what? We call each other by our given names! We all get along regardless of our color. This is the way the world should be. It doesn't matter what race a person is.

When I had cancer and needed surgery, radiation, and chemo, do you think I cared what race the doctor was? Hell no. I just wanted them to save my life and as it turned out, they all worked together to do so. I had a doctor from Vietnam, an oncologist from Pakistan, a Latino screen printer ran my shop while I was gone and a black woman ran the office.

I know people like to associate with like people, but you lose so much when you do that. You never get to know who a person really is if you don't socialize with everyone.

You cannot stop learning in life. I tried to get this kid that worked for me to take classes to learn but he had no desire to learn anything other than what he knew at the time. I would tell him that I was 75 years old and learned something new every day! If I didn't know something, I would look it up. There is no excuse for being ignorant. Reach out to knowledge and to other people. You will be a better person for it and so will the world.

RELIGION

I wasn't going to get into religion, but the recent Supreme Court ruling regarding the enforcement of pandemic rules against churches forces me to do so. They ruled that states could not have different rules for churches than they do shopping centers. This is a stupid ruling by a bunch of religious conservatives on the Supreme Court.

First of all, a person is in a grocery store for a much shorter time than they are in a church and, hopefully, they are not singing in the grocery store and thus spreading the virus all over the place. It is a proven fact that singing in a choir spreads the virus because in Washington state, fifty-two members of a choir came down with the virus after attending a choir get-together.

I should just be mean and say "fine, go ahead and let them spread the virus among themselves if they want to." But they may escape and spread it to innocent people they meet on the way home.

What religious people who are wetting themselves over the things Donald Trump has done for their beliefs fail to take into consideration is this. Your religion may not always be the dominant religion. Islam is growing and is currently 24.6 % of the religions compared to 31.2% for Christianity. All these rules you are putting in place for Christianity may come back to bite you when Islam takes over.

I also disagree with other rulings by prior Supreme Courts when they allowed special rules for religion that do not apply to non-religious businesses. They have allowed religious owned businesses to refuse birth control and abortions to female employees and refuse to provide a service or product to a LGBTQ person. How is that not a law respecting the establishment of a religion? That is forbidden by the First Amendment.

But the most egregious ruling was when Kristen Biel, a teacher at St. James Catholic School in Torrance, CA asked for a leave of absence to undergo a double mastectomy, chemotherapy, and radiation treatments. She asked the school's principal, Sister Mary Margaret Kreuper for a leave and a few weeks later Biel was FIRED! Since then Kristen Biel has died from her cancer. But our Supreme Court ruled that because this was a religious organization, they could fire this woman! For this reason alone, I feel President Biden and the Democrats should pack the court until the court gets this right. This is against anything I was taught as a Christian so how can any of these people call themselves Christians?

I own a custom printed clothing company and years ago, I had stiff competition from a company called TLC. When I looked into why they were able to sell items so much cheaper, I learned that TLC stood for "The Lord's Company." Who would have thought that Jesus was into clothing? My point is that this company was able to compete with my company, but they didn't have to pay taxes. How is this fair?

With the recent pandemic and restaurants in such financial ruin, I suggested in an editorial that they take advantage of the Supreme Court's ruling on allowing churches to admit people, and organize their restaurant as a church. Call it Our Lady of the Perpetual Feast. Not only could they pack in the people, but their income would be tax-exempt. It is a win-win situation!

If a religious non-profit wants to engage in a business in competition with for profit businesses, then they must abide by the same rules. How could the Supreme Court miss this obvious bias in favor or religion?

SOCIAL SECURITY

THE PROBLEMS

After the Great Depression, President Franklin D. Roosevelt realized that workers needed continuing income after they retired. He established the Social Security Act of 1935 which was an insurance plan that paid workers continuing benefits after they retired. This insurance program was paid for by a lifetime tax on earnings. It was called *insurance* not a freebie! Workers paid into the fund all their life through payroll taxes.

Republicans have long resisted increasing deductions for Social Security benefits from paychecks. It will mean that corporations and all businesses will have to pay more in employee taxes. But just like any business that has increased costs (we have more people collecting social security) you have to increase prices or reduce costs to stay in business. We can't reduce costs because we have x number of people who are entitled to x number of dollars per month. Cutting their benefits would be like buying a $10,000 insurance policy and when you go to collect, the company tells you that you are only entitled to $5000.

Another problem is that Social Security payments are based on earnings. The more money you make at your job, the more Social Security benefits you receive. Do you see any problem with that? The problem is that women have always been paid less than men so therefore they will receive less money when they retire. I worked alongside men at CPA firms and earned a lot less than they earned even though I did the same work.

THE SOLUTIONS

Congress needs to increase the cap that is currently on wages subject to Social Security taxes. Currently the cap is $132,900 of income. After that one pays no Social Security tax.

Since we will never know how much a woman WOULD have earned, perhaps the best way to fix this problem is to give women a certain amount in addition to their regular social security payment until such time as Congress fixes the equal pay problem.

WHO WILL OBJECT

Of course, the businesses who pay into social security will object. But let the millionaire CEOs cough up a few more bucks so their employees can afford to live in retirement. The people earning over the $132,900 may complain as well but it is for their own good to ensure that the funds are there when they retire. I am sure most of them are not saving money for retirement and some honestly can't because they can just barely afford to live based on their wages.

TAXES

When our country was founded, the only source of income was from tariffs on products that came from Europe. It wasn't until we got involved in wars that it became necessary to impose a tax on personal income. Finally, in 1913, the Sixteenth Amendment made the income tax permanent. Contrary to what some of your conspiracy theorists believe; it WAS passed and you DO have to pay income taxes.

Over the years taxes have gone from a rate of 3% on income under $60,000 in 1913 to as much as 80% in 1944. Income over $250,000 was taxed at 6% in 1913 and reached a high of 94% in 1944 and is currently at a high of 37%.

Tax codes are worse than a Sudoku puzzle and not nearly as entertaining. The current tax codes are discriminatory in that the tax depends on your career. If you make your money trading stocks, then you pay a lesser rate than the teacher or the firefighter. All those Wall Streeters probably paid less in taxes than you paid.

The tax-exempt entities have scammed the system for years. They have very little accountability and are lax about reporting their income and expenses. I resent that a church can own mansions, yachts, private planes, and the officials take exorbitant salaries, yet pay no taxes. Many of these churches also prey upon the elderly and the poor who can least afford to fund their lavish lifestyles. For example, Trinity Broadcasting Network (TBN) owns a $7.2 million Turbojet, 30 homes, and spent $13.7 million to acquire Twitty City, a tourist attraction. They pay no taxes!

Political tax-exempt corporations should be banned. Period. Trump lost the 2020 election, yet he is still collecting money and so far, has over $200 million in his political fund. He can use that money any way he wants. That is just wrong. I will go a step further and say that the $200 million in that fund should be taken to pay for the destruction to our Capitol that his political action committee supposedly orchestrated.

Corporations receive tax subsidies while earning billions of dollars. We subsidize the oil industry at the same time they are bankrupting us at the pumps. If a corporation can't make it on its own, let it go bankrupt. We need to enforce monopoly laws that prevented corporations from getting too big to fail. We are in this mess because of our so-called representatives who passed these laws that only benefit corporations.

SOLUTION 1 LIMIT EXEMPT INCOME
FOR 501(c)(3) CORPORATIONS

This is a tough one because I do not want to penalize St. Jude Children's Hospital, but I do not want the Catholic Church to molest children and then take a deduction for paying off the victims. They should NOT enjoy tax-exempt status because they hid their employees from prosecution in a court of law for their crimes of rape and child molestation. I wouldn't object to St. Jude's owning a private jet to transport patients and their families, but I do object to Trinity Broadcasting Network owning one to transport their minister to luxury resorts or to one of their 30 homes.

The fair way to handle this is to limit the exemption to those non-profits that provide an actual service to the public. Simple getting up in front of a crowd on Sunday morning is not a service to the public.

Sorry. Providing a hospital or a homeless shelter IS a service. Only that part of a religious institution should be tax-exempt.

I feel I can speak out against the benefits religion enjoys at our expense because I come from a religious background. I am appalled at what I see churches doing and I can't understand why you aren't appalled also. I was brought up in as Baptist in Ohio. Then I was confirmed in the Lutheran Church. Then I was baptized at Rex Humbard's Cathedral of Tomorrow in Akron Ohio. When I moved to California, I taught Sunday School at Robert Schuller's Crystal Cathedral and finally taught Sunday School at Hollywood Presbyterian Church when Lloyd Ogilvie was the pastor. But I must have read a different Bible because mine said "what you have done unto the least of mine, you have done unto me."

At the very least, a church that hides molesters and refuses to obey the government laws should lose their tax-exempt status. Yet once again **fear sells** and they threaten legislators so that everyone leaves them alone. They are no better than the thug on the corner. I would NEVER give money to a church that molests my children. But then that's just me! I acknowledge that Jesus forgave sinners but he also said, "Go and sin no more!" I looked everywhere and I couldn't find a single instance where Jesus said, "See ya tomorrow!"

Many of your representatives use the 501(c)(3) status to set up their own non-profits where they employ family members. Their corporate contributors than make huge donations to the representative's non-profit and get a write-off for it.

The IRS does little to reign in this abuse. The only way to stop it is to, well, STOP IT! There needs to be limits on the salaries of non-profit corporations and assets need to be limited to those necessary for the operation of the service provided. Everything else gets taxed. We are losing BILLIONS OF DOLLARS to sham non-profits. Just by stopping this abuse, we can probably pay down much of our national debt.

If a non-profit is going to engage in competition with businesses that DO pay taxes, then they have to operate under the same rules and pay taxes as well on those earnings and cannot be a (501C(3) corporation.

In 2009 there were 1,581,111 non-profit organizations filed with the IRS. If they each paid only $1,000 in taxes, that would be over $1.5 billion to help pay down the debt per year!

SOLUTION 2 FLAT TAX

Once all the other changes are made (corruption, fraud, and incompetency) we should be able to determine a reasonable budget and then institute a flat tax on income. Those earning under a certain amount should be exempt from taxes.

SOLUTION 3 CONSUMPTION TAX

The consumption tax is a tax that you pay when you purchase something, much like the sales taxes that states charge. It could work if it exempted food, clothing, and housing from the tax. If you don't do this, then you will unfairly tax the poor.

SOLUTION 4 CAPITAL GAINS TAX

There is a serious problem with Capital Gains Taxes. If you derive all your income from the stock market it is still considered Capital Gains and is taxed at a lower rate than if you make your living from a salaried or hourly job. That is simply wrong. Just because you only trade in stocks shouldn't give you a tax break over everyone else.

Therefore, if more than 10% of your income comes from Capital Gains, the excess amount is considered ordinary income and taxed at the same rate as salaried or hourly wage earners. This will add considerable income to pay down our national debt and equalize our tax system.

VOTING

I am always amazed when I go to the polls that I am never asked for any identification. I bring my driver's license but have never been asked for it. I have my voting pamphlet with me but anyone, had I dropped it, could have picked it up and voted in my place. While I have to sign my name, even I don't always sign my name the same. It depends upon how hurried I am. This year when we were voting by computer, I had to sign my name with a soft-tipped squishy pen and even I didn't recognize my signature. So, if they were comparing it to anything, my vote would have been thrown out.

We need to get over the propaganda that requiring a national ID is an infringement on our rights and a sinister plot to take away our rights. It is only COMMON SENSE to have a national ID. This would allow you to vote, obtain Social Security and Medicare benefits, and file taxes. It should contain your thumb print and name and address plus your ID number. It is more likely to be kept up to date by the holder because you will need your current address to access benefits. Thus, voter logs will no longer have multiple addresses for the same person.

When George W. Bush was running for President, the company Diebold was bidding on the contract for voting machines and is alleged to have said, "Give me the contract and we will give you the election." Whether that was true or not, I don't know. Given that Dick Cheney was running the country then, it probably was true. Either way, electronic voting is simply not secure. If hackers can get into the Pentagon computers, then they can get into any computer.

It is disputably said that Soviet dictator, Joseph Stalin, said, "*Those who vote decide nothing. Those who count the votes decide everything.*" Whoever said it, it makes sense.

They tried everything in 2020 to get people to vote. Some used special boxes for people to drop their ballots in much like a mail box. It doesn't take a brainiac to figure out that those boxes in minority area could be ripped up out of the cement in the night and disposed of. The most secure vote is in person and allowing people extra days to vote and conducting the voting on a weekend could increase voting.

If you want to get more people voting, then make it more convenient. Many older people don't know how to use the computers. I know how to use them, but I often, especially at the grocery store, hit the wrong keys and end up somewhere or with something I didn't buy. I am very impatient and when it kept asking me how many mushrooms I had, I hit six. But when it asked again, I entered six again and ended up paying for 66 mushrooms! One could easily vote for someone or something you don't want by using the computer.

In addition to the voting ID issue, we also need a requirement for passing a civics test before you can vote. You have to know how the government works or you can't vote responsibly.

I would rather have 100 people vote who understand the issues than 10,000 who vote based on a two-minute TV ad or something they read on the internet. Remember, George Washington said **"Every right has a responsibility."** So yes, you have the right to vote, but you have the responsibility to learn about what you are voting for or against.

SOLUTION

The best way to have secure voting is with a national ID card and paper ballots. If a computer malfunctions (and we have all had our computers eat up data never to be seen again), the info is lost forever. But if you have paper ballots, you can have a recount, if necessary, and you have a permanent record that cannot be manipulated. It may be old fashioned, but it works!

Devise a simple civics test that the voter has to turn in when they vote and if they don't pass a simple test of understanding how your government works, then you can't vote. Better yet, give voters the same test we do to people wanting to become citizens! We'll probably be lucky to get a hundred thousand people eligible to vote.

The best solution is to start a third party so that one party is not in control. That is just common sense and you need to get rid of the idea that there can only be two parties. It isn't like they are aliens from Mars landing and starting a party. These are people with common sense who want to solve our problems, not make money off of them. But common sense is misnamed. It is not that common. It should be called "uncommon sense."

THE PANDEMIC

I would be remiss if I didn't address the corona virus pandemic because there is a huge lesson to be learned from it and if you learn from it, then it was not in vain and would have been well worth the suffering. But if you don't' learn, then it was a horrible waste of lives.

Most importantly, the pandemic taught us how everyone that we have been paying huge salaries to all these years for their *expertise* were lying to us. They didn't have any more *expertise* than we do. The CEO's of the airlines who have been earning from $8 to $14 million a year, were like deer in the headlights when the pandemic hit. They, of all people, were almost single handedly responsible for the transmission of the virus because they failed to take any precautions when flying their passengers around the world. To this day, they still balk at taking the very basic precautions to prevent the spread and still want to jam people into these virus spreaders called airplanes.

Next was the World Health Organization and the Center For Disease Control for their failure to act quickly and non-prejudicially warn the world about the risk. The WHO allowed China to control the amount of information getting out about the virus when it originated in China. Then almost a year later, the WHO goes to the Chinese city where the virus was believed to have originated, and conducts an inspection! Really? A year later? Plus, they only relied on the information China gave them and did not conduct their own investigation.

The pandemic has actually worked to the advantage of the corporations. Aside from the billions of stimulus money they received, the received a plethora of benefits from the pandemic. They have employees working from home and like good sheeple, they do so at no cost to their employer. Even worse, the IRS doesn't allow them to deduct the cost of the area in their homes where they work, unless they do so as a contractor and not an employee. So, corporations need less office space and don't have all the other expenses of having employees on site.

Grocery stores now charge you for your grocery bags. More stores have opened self-check-out lines so they will need less employees. Once again, it is YOU, the consumer, who suffers the most.

I could go on and on but basically the blame lies with everyone from the president of the U.S. and everyone in the chain all the way down to the local health departments.

What it should teach us is that we need to take our pay pyramid in the world and turn it upside down. The people getting all the big bucks don't deserve it and the people at the bottom are really the *essential workers* – not the CEOs. The healthcare workers, the grocery workers, the truckers, and the teachers, who had to jump into the pool with no one telling them how to swim, are the ones who should be paid the big bucks. Teachers should be at the top for the obvious reason – **no one learns how to do what they do in life without a teacher somewhere in your life who made it possible.**

Pay Pyramid

(The way it SHOULD be)

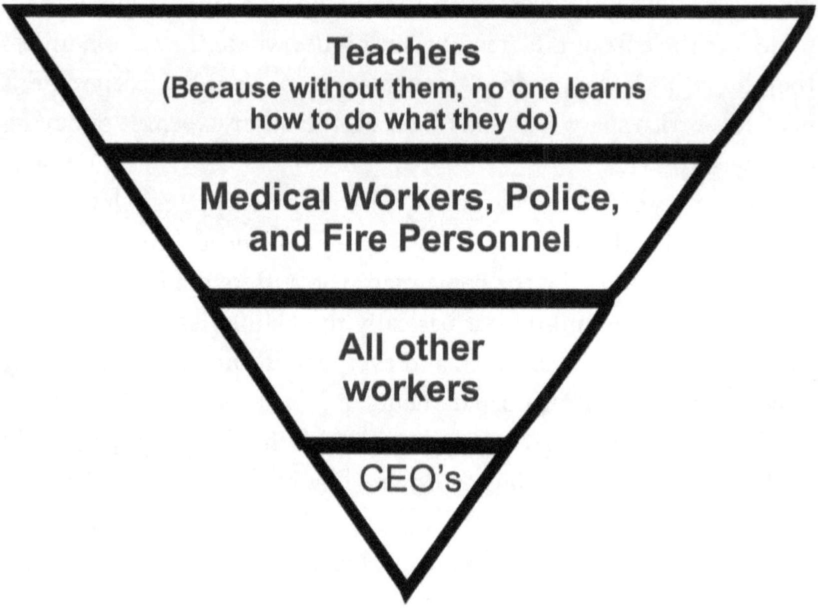

Figure 3PAY PYRAMID

HOW THE BOOK SHOULD WORK

I don't just criticize. I offer solutions also. Any fool can criticize but a smart person offers solutions to the problems.

Let me give you an example. In my neighborhood, the Golden State Water Company would graffiti the sidewalks with the location of their pipes and controls. I wrote to Robert Sprowls, the head of Golden State Water and suggested that he put permanent markers on the top of the curb. I suggested a license plate like marker so that every time they had to dig up the street, they didn't have to call a survey team to come out and mark up our sidewalks. Well he not only took my suggestion, but went one better. He put small tiles with a "V" for Valve on the top of the curbs wherever the valves were located. Much better looking than a license plate and longer lasting. I might add also, that Mr. Sprowls is a smart executive and worthy of his salary, because he LISTENED to his customer and got free advice. Others would have hired a research company, paid them millions, and probably not done as well as Mr. Sprowls did in solving the problem.

The object of this book is to take my suggestions and build on them and make them better. I can't possibly have all the answers but I can at least get you thinking about productive solutions and not just complaining. NEVER COMPLAIN WITHOUT OFFERING A VIABLE SOLUTION!

First, start a website and get people to vote on the issues that are most important. As I have said, the first issue to resolve is the limit on campaign contributions. If you don't do that, you may as well forget about anything else because our current politicians are too accustomed to taking bribes.

Then decide on a name for the party. Stay away from names that can be misconstrued by the other two parties and backfire. For example, no People's Party, as they will claim it is a Communist party. But you could use the Human Party because you are representing human people and not corporate people as the Republican Party does.

Once you have agreed on the issues, then file as a new political party in all states and districts so you can promote candidates from the party.

Next begin promotions of the third party on all media. The goal is to have the party so well-known that you don't have to advertise. All people have to do is recognize the party affiliated with your candidate and know what they stand for and vote for the candidate in your party

You won't need a presidential candidate the first time out because if you choose the wrong one, you will doom the party. Go for local, state, and federal representation instead. After your candidates perform for a term, look for a presidential candidate from that group.

But most importantly, GET STARTED! YOU have to take action.

As Amanda Gorman, the brilliant young poet said at President Biden's inauguration, ***"There is always light if only we're brave enough to see it, if only we're brave enough to be it."***

ABOUT THE AUTHOR

Shirley Conley has been a small business owner since 1982 and has kept her business alive through numerous recessions and competition. She has survived due to her ability to organize, see the whole picture, and act to solve issues. She was executive director of Victims for Victims, a nonprofit organization founded by actress Theresa Saldana after she was brutally stabbed by a crazed fan. She also brought together the leaders of other victims' groups to pass legislation called the Victims Bill of Rights in California. She organized the first Candlelight Vigil for Crime Victims for the Sunny von Bulow Victim Advocacy Center.

www.ingramcontent.com/pod-product-compliance
Lightning Source LLC
Chambersburg PA
CBHW031135250726
48655CB00002B/676